"No one writing today has seen the necessary intersection of psychoanalysis and deconstruction more lucidly and comprehensively than Jared Russell. Discussing a wide range of psychoanalytic writers, Russell provides an essential education in how and why these bodies of thought have always been in dialogue, and how and why the future of psychoanalysis depends upon this dialogue. This is a must read for anyone working in these fields."

**Alan Bass**, New School for Social Research, New York City, USA

"In *Psychoanalysis and Deconstruction: Freud's Psychic Apparatus*, Jared Russell adeptly brings together psychoanalysis and deconstruction to demonstrate how the Freudian concept of a psychic apparatus takes into account, from the beginning, a notion of the incalculable. In lucid prose that places clinical vignettes alongside readings in deconstruction on the question of the machine, technicity, temporality, and life, Russell offers his readers a glimpse of a contemporary psychoanalytic clinic informed by the lessons of deconstruction. In doing so, Russell on the one hand opens up the field of deconstruction to the practice of psychoanalysis, and on the other opens psychoanalysis, in its contemporary iteration, to an important critique by deconstructive thought."

**Azeen A. Khan**, Dartmouth College, Hanover, New Hampshire, USA

"In an extraordinary work of deep reflection, Jared Russell offers an effective reading experiment with a remarkable outcome. Russell reads deconstruction and psychoanalysis alongside one another to rehabilitate a Freudian materialistic vocabulary that psychoanalysts have wrongly abandoned. Focusing on Derrida's reading of Freud, which (re)thinks the psyche as a machine, Russell makes a significant contribution to bringing psychoanalysis and philosophy together. He offers a deeper understanding of the practice of psychoanalysis, and of the philosophical grasp of the relationship between mind and subject."

**Rosaura Martínez-Ruiz**, National Autonomous University of Mexico, Mexico City, Mexico

# PSYCHOANALYSIS AND DECONSTRUCTION

*Psychoanalysis and Deconstruction: Freud's Psychic Apparatus* demonstrates the relevance of deconstructive thinking for the clinical practice of psychoanalysis. Arguing that deconstruction has been misrepresented as a form of literary theory or a philosophy of language, the book puts Derrida, Heidegger and others working in the tradition of deconstruction into dialogue with debates in the contemporary psychoanalytic field.

Attempting to retrieve what was radical in Freud's portrayal of the mind as a machine, Jared Russell stresses the importance of psychoanalysis for an understanding of the relationship between the human and its current hyper-technological environment. Interventions into contemporary debates address psychoanalytic concepts such as the nature of the clinical frame, the intersubjective dialogue, unconscious communication and the experience of time. Russell argues that deconstruction, and in particular Derrida's work, can anticipate and help clarify ongoing developments at the cutting edge of psychoanalysis today.

*Psychoanalysis and Deconstruction: Freud's Psychic Apparatus* will appeal not only to a philosophically informed audience but also to clinicians attempting to secure a place for psychoanalytic practice at the beginning of the twenty-first century.

**Jared Russell, PhD,** is a psychoanalyst in private practice in New York City, USA. He is Managing Editor of *The Undecidable Unconscious: A Journal of Deconstruction and Psychoanalysis* (University of Nebraska Press) and the author of *Nietzsche and the Clinic: Psychoanalysis, Philosophy, Metaphysics* (Routledge, 2016).

# PSYCHOANALYSIS AND DECONSTRUCTION

Freud's Psychic Apparatus

Jared Russell

LONDON AND NEW YORK

First published 2020
by Routledge
2 Park Square, Milton Park, Abingdon, Oxon OX14 4RN

and by Routledge
52 Vanderbilt Avenue, New York, NY 10017

*Routledge is an imprint of the Taylor & Francis Group, an informa business*

© 2020 Jared Russell

The right of Jared Russell to be identified as author of this work has been asserted by him in accordance with sections 77 and 78 of the Copyright, Designs and Patents Act 1988.

All rights reserved. No part of this book may be reprinted or reproduced or utilised in any form or by any electronic, mechanical, or other means, now known or hereafter invented, including photocopying and recording, or in any information storage or retrieval system, without permission in writing from the publishers.

*Trademark notice*: Product or corporate names may be trademarks or registered trademarks, and are used only for identification and explanation without intent to infringe.

*British Library Cataloguing-in-Publication Data*
A catalogue record for this book is available from the British Library

*Library of Congress Cataloging-in-Publication Data*
Names: Russell, Jared, author.
Title: Psychoanalysis and deconstruction : Freud's psychic apparatus / Jared Russell.
Description: Abingdon, Oxon ; New York, NY : Routledge, 2019. |
Includes bibliographical references and index.
Identifiers: LCCN 2019009325 (print) | LCCN 2019011233 (ebook) |
ISBN 9780429289927 (Master) | ISBN 9781000020823 (Adobe) |
ISBN 9781000020991 (Mobipocket) | ISBN 9781000021165 (ePub) |
ISBN 9780367257958 (hardback : alk. paper) |
ISBN 9780367257972 (pbk. : alk. paper)
Subjects: LCSH: Psychoanalysis. | Psychotherapy. | Deconstruction.
Classification: LCC BF173 (ebook) |
LCC BF173 .R884 2019 (print) | DDC 150.19/5–dc23
LC record available at https://lccn.loc.gov/2019009325

ISBN: 978-0-367-25795-8 (hbk)
ISBN: 978-0-367-25797-2 (pbk)
ISBN: 978-0-429-28992-7 (ebk)

Typeset in Bembo
by Newgen Publishing UK

For Sonja

# CONTENTS

| | | |
|---|---|---|
| *Acknowledgments* | | *xi* |
| Introduction | | 1 |
| 1 | Differance and psychic space | 13 |
| 2 | The spectrality of the clinical frame | 35 |
| 3 | A new metrics of clinical time | 71 |
| 4 | Psychoanalysis and pharmacology | 95 |
| *Postscript: The trauma of the clinic of the telepathic machine* | | *121* |
| *Index* | | *129* |

# ACKNOWLEDGMENTS

For their friendship and support during the writing of this project I would like to thank my colleagues Alan Bass, Melissa Daum, Steven Ellman, Anna Fishzon, Gerald Gargiulo, Matthew Hackett, Warren Holt, Yunus Tuncel, Jamieson Webster and Yukari Yanagino. Friendship is, by definition, too rare.

An earlier version of Chapter 1 appeared as "Differance and Psychic Space." Copyright © Johns Hopkins University Press. This article was first published in *American Imago* 60.4 (2003), 501–528. Reprinted with permission by Johns Hopkins University Press. An earlier version of Chapter 3 appeared as "Deconstruction and the Metrics of Clinical Time," in *The Undecidable Unconscious: A Journal of Deconstruction and Psychoanalysis*, 3. Reprinted with permission by University of Nebraska Press. An earlier version of Chapter 4 appeared as "Stiegler and the Clinic," in *The Undecidable Unconscious: A Journal of Deconstruction and Psychoanalysis*, 2. Reprinted with permission by University of Nebraska Press. Sections of Chapters 2 and 4 appeared in "Training and time," *The Candidate Journal: Psychoanalytic Currents* 7, 2017: 8–15. Reprinted with kind permission.

# INTRODUCTION

There is a scene in Kirby Dick and Amy Ziering's 2002 biographical documentary *Derrida* that I find fascinating. It shows Derrida being interviewed on a British television program. The interviewer asks an innocent yet uninformed question about deconstruction, bumbling through an allusion to the American situation comedy program *Seinfeld* and suggesting that deconstruction is similar in that it is primarily concerned with how nothing ultimately means anything more than anything else. With a puzzled look on his face, Derrida pauses just long enough to make the moment uncomfortable, before gently telling his interviewer, "If that is what you imagine deconstruction is... stop watching sitcoms and read."

It is an intriguing moment at the very least for the fact that it is perhaps the only moment on record where Derrida appears tempted for once to abandon his characteristic generosity and to be simply rude in telling someone that they have no idea what they are talking about. He manages to defer that impulse, but the look on his face indicates that he does so with some difficulty. Beyond the dynamics of that particular moment, I am always tempted to read in the look Derrida gives the trace of his experience of his own public reputation. In a flash he appears burdened by the history of the encounter between his name and the popular imagination—that vast population of enthusiasts and detractors who were for some reason, and who remain to this day, prone to speaking of him in public without having taken the slightest amount of time to actually read and to work through his writings, much less the voluminous writings of those authors about whom he wrote voluminously. When he passed away in 2004, the title of his obituary on the front page of *The New York Times* announced, "Abstruse Theorist Dies." It was not difficult to hear the barb in these words, but at the same time it was not an inaccurate assessment, and so doubly strange was it then that his death would receive such publicity. In a manner that Derrida himself would no doubt have found fascinating, this

**2** Introduction

announcement had demonstrated how an effort to memorialize can also function as a gesture of erasure.

In a series of interviews conducted with Elisabeth Roudinesco which appeared in English translation the year of his death, Derrida and his interlocutor commiserated over the backlash against what had come to be known in France, after the title of Luc Ferry and Alain Renaut's popular 1990 book, as "French Philosophy of the Sixties" (*La Penseé '68*). The book had attacked not only Derrida, but virtually all of the intellectuals of his generation. Inspired by a resurgent nationalism (Derrida was denounced as "The French Heidegger," Foucault as "The French Nietzsche," Bourdieu as "The French Marx," and Lacan as "The French Freud"—traitors who had dared to import German culture into the French university system), Ferry and Renaut's criticisms appealed to a wide audience precisely due to their lack of critical rigor. For those looking for an excuse precisely not to do the work of reading, the book confirmed their suspicions about what these authors' works contained and about what contemporary social ills could be blamed on their influence. Derrida was singled out with a particular amount of venom. There was a more general precedence to this targeting, and to Roudinesco he rightly complained, "I am obliged to claim an unfortunate privilege here: I seem to attract a more stubborn and relentless aggression" (2004, p. 3).

Ironically, those uninformed critics who are quick today to denounce the influence of "French philosophy" in the British and American universities are repeating this same gesture which began in France as a thinly-concealed accusation of Germanism. The right routinely accuses left-wing intellectuals of having taken over the culture of the contemporary university system by promoting "postmodernism," as if this named an ideology produced by some highly coordinated think tank located somewhere in Paris. Meanwhile, the left has for just as long portrayed these very same authors as being not only anti-democratic but sympathetic to Nazism (following the "affairs" of Heidegger and Paul de Man). Denouncing a caricature often called "deconstructionism" (the word itself betrays the incompetence of the critique) is the common ground that today unites leftist ultra-contrarians like Slavoj Žižek with right-wing motivational speakers like Jordan Peterson.[1]

What is being attacked under these conditions is not deconstruction, at least not as it was practiced by Derrida, but a previously glamorous yet distorted version of deconstruction that had been popularized for the most part by college professors working in university departments associated with cultural studies. It was from there that deconstruction, often taken to be simply synonymous with the ill-defined "postmodern" attitude, was promoted as a discourse of radical relativism that refused as authoritarian any traditional values or any investments in European history and culture. As had happened to Nietzsche with the Nazis, and as the American Psychiatric Association had done with Freud, Derrida's name and the project with which it was associated were widely coopted and misrepresented, in this case by an unbridled spirit of liberal humanism posing as informed philosophical critique. Derrida had made no secret of his unwavering commitment to democracy, but deconstruction was interpreted as if it meant that anything claiming to be of particular historical or cultural significance and value was to be absolutely opposed and taken to task. In many quarters, again especially on North American university campuses, this attitude authorized what would become the culture of political correctness and, more recently, of identity politics—an anti-deconstructive practice if ever there was one.[2]

In reality, Derrida was always far from being an enemy of the Western European tradition. With Roudinesco he summarized his position rather eloquently as that of someone "who is dying to be unfaithful in a spirit of fidelity… My desire resembles that of a lover of the tradition who would like to free himself of conservatism" (2004, pp. 3–4). It was this desire to inherit the Western canon, and to do so in the spirit of that canon so as to reject its nostalgic or totalitarian closure, that had defined Derrida's work all along. And it was precisely this desire that Derrida shared with—perhaps above all others—Heidegger, Nietzsche and Freud, who would be the most important and influential figures in the formulation of the project of deconstruction.

It is difficult today to appreciate just how much Derrida's willingness to engage in an affirmative and original way with psychoanalysis set him apart from his contemporaries (with the major exception, of course, of Lacan). Those who currently work in the critical traditions inaugurated by Foucault and Deleuze, for example, are rarely as hostile towards psychoanalysis as these authors were themselves, at least in their more famous publications. Those academics of Derrida's generation who were attracted to psychoanalysis almost exclusively took their orientation from Lacan's ("French") reading of Freud as against the authoritarianism of what had come to call itself psychoanalysis in the form of the governing bureaucracy of the International Psychoanalytic Association (IPA). As a general cultural trend at that particular time and place in intellectual history, either one was against Freudian psychoanalysis, or one was against psychoanalysis in favor of Freud.

In his early readings of Freud, Derrida did not politicize his relationship to psychoanalysis in this way. He was not concerned with taking up a position for or against psychoanalysis regarded as a singular, coherent orthodoxy. Instead, Derrida saw that this discourse inaugurated by Freud was wildly complex and self-contradictory, often containing profound philosophical insights of which it was entirely oblivious, or announcing new strategies of liberation haunted by the worst reactionary logics. Protecting himself from the charge of practicing a "psychoanalysis of philosophy" (1978, p. 196), Derrida put Freud's efforts to establish an anti-metaphysical psychological science into dialogue with Heidegger's attempt at a "destruction" (*Destruktion*) of metaphysics, and with Nietzsche's anti-Platonic efforts to "philosophize with a hammer." This was, roughly, the elementary matrix from out of which deconstruction would be formulated and that would distinguish Derrida's textual practice from so many others working at the time.

This is also what gives Derrida's work (particularly in what might be called, in a highly provisional and artificial manner, his "middle phase"—I am thinking of texts such as *Dissemination* (1981), *The Post Card* (1987), and *Glas* (1990) which are more recognizably experimental in nature than his densely academic early essays and his

**4** Introduction

more relaxed, almost conversational later work) a certain high modern style, and which accounts for its stylistic difficulty at times. Like many French intellectuals of his generation who had achieved some degree of fame outside the academy, and who were working in a cultural milieu highly overdetermined by the aftereffects of Breton's surrealism, Derrida experimented with the style of textual arguments and with the organizational structure of printed documents. His reputation for being inscrutably difficult among philosophers is in many respects due to his having occasionally deployed stylistic practices that had made Stephane Mallarmé and James Joyce famous as celebrated writers of poetry and fiction, and that would not have been nearly so confounding to generations raised on consuming information from the Internet.

The truly unique Derridean gesture, in the midst of a culture that was widely experimenting with techniques of writing, was to have put the question as to the nature of writing itself at the center of the discourse he was assembling. Derrida was a writer who wrote about writing. That he did so does not make him unique, but that he did so as a classically trained European academic, and in order to place academic philosophy, in a turn of phrase now associated with his name, *"en abyme"*— in a position such that it could become capable of reflecting on itself intensively, in order to see that there were things it could not see about itself, to account for its own inherent failures and blindspots—was an extremely original and powerful project at a particular moment in intellectual history. It is also why he knew that deconstruction might be misconstrued as a "psychoanalysis of philosophy."

One of the reasons this charge would have been inadequate had to do with the way in which Derrida approached the textual history of psychoanalysis itself. Quite like Lacan, Derrida practiced a return to a rigorous reading of Freud's texts in order to recuperate something that the analytic tradition had glossed over and forgotten. Unlike Lacan, Derrida's strategy—what would come to be considered the strategy that defines the project of deconstruction—was to tend to apparently minor texts that the tradition had either forgotten or not invested much in to begin with. Lacan's strategy was to reread major texts in the Freudian canon and to demonstrate how these had been read superficially by the progenitors of the IPA, including, at times, Freud himself (this is not an unreasonable claim, even if one does not tend to agree with Lacan's own readings of that canon). Derrida's approach was to locate minor texts (the *Project for a Scientific Psychology* of 1895, the essays on "The Uncanny" and "Telepathy," the "Note on the Mystic Writing Pad," etc.) which proved capable—by means of a reading of that which the tradition of institutionalized psychoanalysis had depended upon yet had not deemed worthy of attention—of recasting the ways in which Freud's more familiar and canonical texts should be approached. Deconstruction was in this sense not a hypercritical effort to dismantle an author's claims, rather it was an affirmative effort to renew the foundational act of *reading* in the context of entrenched orthodoxies.

By means of this concern for the centrality of the marginal, and beginning in 1966 with what would become "Freud and the Scene of Writing" (his first major statement concerning psychoanalysis, and perhaps still his most important), Derrida had recovered the importance for Freud of conceiving of the mind as a *machine*, and particularly as a *writing* machine, according to a metaphor that, as Derrida demonstrated, Freud could not escape, and one that challenges any ordinary consideration of metaphor as a figure of mere representation. I will leave it to the reader to discover in the chapters that follow why it should be considered radical for Freud to have thought of the mind as a machine in the way that Derrida had recognized, beyond any opposition between the organic and the technological. My hope is that over the course of reading the present text the significance of its title gradually will become apparent. The history of psychoanalysis has largely been figured as a move away from this analogy, away from concepts that were central both to Freud and to Derrida: force, energy, trace, drive, mechanism, apparatus. Contemporary psychoanalysis regards these terms as anachronistic, belonging to an outmoded way of thinking that modeled itself on nineteenth-century physical science. In 1983 the American psychiatrist Merton Gill posed the question, "The point of view of psychoanalysis: energy discharge or person?" This signaled the triumphant return to an uncritical humanism incapable of accounting for a concept like the Freudian unconscious, and incapable of conceiving of a psychoanalytic practice outside the bounds of a traditionally authoritarian conservatism—one that is very confident in its knowledge of true human nature.[3]

While psychoanalysis has been busy congratulating itself for having rejected its earlier incarnations in favor of humanistic appeals to empathy, co-construction and maternalism, cognitive science has given rise to an international campaign dedicated to enforcing a phallic image of mind as comparable to the computer, and of thinking as identical to digital computation. This too is a metaphor, yet one that now governs a global industry capable of authorizing massive economic investments in itself in the name of science and of progress. This can only be because there is something relevant in the machine metaphor, something that psychoanalysis rejects to the detriment of its own continued relevance.

A psychoanalytic approach informed by deconstruction would allow us to be done with the exhausted opposition between humanism and technological rationality and to ask, not whether or not the mind is a machine, but if it is comparable to a machine then what kind of machine must it be? A computational machine that is fundamentally closed off from the world about which it is capable only of taking in and processing information? Or a machine that is fundamentally open to the world in a way that is dynamically self-organizing? Would a machine of this kind be unnatural and supplementary to the living organism, or would it be part of an intrinsically natural process by means of which nature reveals itself as a process of becoming other than or of differentiating itself? And what exactly is a machine if it bears the traces of, so as to be capable of symbolizing, the human mind?

In Chapter 1 I introduce key Derridean concepts and themes, with an emphasis on the famous neologism *différance* given the privilege this term has been accorded in the reception of Derrida's work. Simultaneously this chapter also takes up the psychoanalytic notion of "psychic space," particularly as it is to be found in the

**6** Introduction

writings of Donald Winnicott and of Thomas Ogden. Looking closely at the ways in which spatial and temporal metaphors circulate in any discussion of psychic interiority leads me to an opening where it is possible to begin thinking about what Derrida intended to indicate, and in terms that are relevant to clinical practice. A comparison of Derrida's "*différance*" with Winnicott's notion of "playing"— a notion that is far more philosophically sophisticated than Winnicott is often given credit for in the psychoanalytic literature—develops along lines of intersection between Derrida's thinking about intermediary, non-dialectical processes and Winnicott's thinking about transitionality. Putting Derrida into dialogue with Winnicott also opens some potentially powerful avenues for rethinking the developmental nature of the mother-infant matrix and the status of the infantile mind in the context of this primitive, pre-subjective relation. Insights into this dynamic yet non-metaphysical relation are then carried over to a thinking about the analytic clinical relationship as an effort at helping the patient to cultivate a capacity for symbolization. I also begin an effort that continues throughout subsequent chapters to reconsider the relationship between what psychoanalysis means by symbolization and what is referred to more generally as cognition.

Chapter 1 is not intended to be a broad overview of all of Derrida's contributions, or even those of his texts that deal directly with the topic of psychoanalysis. Instead, my effort is to show where there are moments in Derrida's writings that are incontestably similar to moments in the psychoanalytic literature, in order to begin to read deconstruction and psychoanalysis alongside one another and in order to see what happens as a result. This will be my strategy throughout the book. Should the philosophically informed reader occasionally find some passages rather basic, rest assured that the clinically experienced reader will undoubtedly feel the same way at times, and that this is inevitably what happens when a space for genuine dialogue is opened up. Readers anticipating a comparison of the respective theories of deconstruction and of psychoanalysis in the manner of an academic textbook will be disappointed. Those open to thinking adventurously about what happens when we entertain certain proximities of deconstructive and psychoanalytic thinking hopefully will not.

Chapter 2 is organized around a consideration of what is meant by the "frame" in psychoanalysis—that is, in the theory of psychoanalytic practice, which is not always commensurate with that practice itself. Drawing on concepts elaborated in Chapter 1, this chapter extends those concepts further by developing an understanding of Derrida's expanded notion of "writing" and of the theme of "spectrality" which emerges in his later work. It is also here, early in the chapter, that an appreciation of Heidegger's thinking as it relates to deconstruction and to questions about the nature of the analytic frame is undertaken and which will be further pursued and developed in the course of the remaining chapters. As many writers on the topic have intuited, there is something about the clinical frame that necessarily implicates a kind of "existential" thinking. It requires working through basic concepts in Heidegger's work to understand why this is and what this means.

With regard to the psychoanalytic literature, Chapter 2 examines Marion Milner's crucial contributions to discussions of the clinical frame. It is not often enough recalled that it was Milner who first introduced the very concept, and in some ways she is still the author to have said the most interesting things about it, despite how little she wrote on the topic. Having deduced the concept of the clinical frame from an analogy to the frame in painting and in the work of art, Milner's comments on the frame invite more general philosophical reflections on the work of psychoanalysis, and that are not limited to that branch of academic philosophy to which a thinking about the work of art is typically assigned (i.e. aesthetics). The vocabulary and even the set of references that Milner deploys are strikingly similar to those used by Derrida, whose *The Truth in Painting* (1987) is also a meditation on the frame and its relation to the *work* of art understood as the undecidable boundary between the materialized art object and the activity (which can sometimes feel strangely passive) of artistic production.

The most substantial section of Chapter 2 concerns the seminal essay "Psycho-Analysis of the Psycho-Analytic Frame" (1967) by the Argentinian analyst José Bleger. Bleger, whose work is beginning to generate some interest in North America, was a fascinating analytic thinker whose work appears deeply philosophically informed to the trained reader. His essay on the clinical frame reads as if it were in direct dialogue with themes that Derrida was developing at the same time on the European continent, and it anticipates the distinctly Derridean theme of spectrality as a way of thinking about ghosts, memory, institutions, traditions, space and time. Of all the sections in the book this one is perhaps the most incomplete, as there will undoubtedly be much more to say in the future about Bleger's work and its implications for a psychoanalysis that takes philosophy seriously. Fittingly then, Chapter 2 concludes with a brief consideration of a passage from the work of Hans Loewald—another analyst about whose relationship to philosophy much still remains to be said—that intersects with everything indicated by Milner, Bleger and Derrida about the clinical frame as a form of spectral "technology."

Chapter 3 deepens the analysis of Heidegger's thinking as it relates both to deconstruction and to a certain discourse that is beginning to emerge in disparate corners of the contemporary psychoanalytic literature concerning the clinical experience of time. Heidegger's specific and expanded understanding of what "thinking" consists in is developed as an anticipation of Derrida's expanded, non-metaphysical concept of "writing," which is crucial to an understanding of what is meant by "deconstruction." Pursuing the question of the meaning of the possibility of writing via Freud's writings on the topic of telepathy, Derrida offers some difficult but suggestive comments in his essay "Telepathy" (2007) that pertain to Freud's having conceived of the unconscious analytic relationship at one point on the model of the apparatus of the telephone. This conception is also central to the work of Christopher Bollas, whose efforts to rehabilitate the practices of free association and evenly suspended attention bear a distinctly Derridean trace.

As Chapter 2 brings to the fore the work of José Bleger whose profound philosophical insights into the psychoanalytic process do not warrant his relative

**8** Introduction

obscurity outside of his native Argentina, Chapter 3 takes up writing by the contemporary British Kleinian analyst Dana Birksted-Breen whose reputation similarly needs to be announced to the wider psychoanalytic and philosophical communities. The extent to which Birksted-Breen's work communicates with themes central to the analyses of both Heidegger and Derrida is at times simply staggering, all the more so because at no point does she give any indication that she is in the least bit familiar with their work. Birksted-Breen offers what I consider to be the most sophisticated account of what a fully articulated psychoanalytic theory of time might look like (she is far in advance of the few hints that Loewald gave us). Even more impressively, she uses this thinking about time to justify the classical analytic stance and to criticize those innumerable approaches today that focus insistently on the here-and-now of the transference. Through a descriptive clinical theory of time or of temporal experience in psychoanalysis, Birksted-Breen puts together in new ways a dynamic theory of mind with an eminently practical theory of clinical intervention. It is not clear to me whether she is aware of just how considerable is her accomplishment here. I hope to draw attention to the sophistication of her thinking by pointing to its intrinsically, intuitively deconstructive dimension.

Finally, Chapter 4 represents somewhat of a departure, which I intend as an opening toward potentially new forms of critical-clinical discourse. With Heidegger's and Derrida's projects in the background, as always, this concluding chapter begins with a reading of Freud's *Civilization and Its Discontents* (1930) that emphasizes those passages where Freud inadvertently outlines a specifically psychoanalytic thinking about technology—an aspect of the text for which it is not often remembered. This reading also emphasizes the clinical relevance of *Civilization and Its Discontents* as a text primarily concerned with what Freud calls "techniques in the art of living," and for which it deserves a careful and updated rereading by contemporary clinicians. I demonstrate that the manner in which Freud thinks about technology in this text and from a specifically psychoanalytic point of view bears a distinct resemblance to the logic of deconstruction, for which, and despite its erroneous reputation as a form of literary analysis or as a philosophy of language, a critical thinking about the relationship between the human and the technical is absolutely central. The importance of thinking both psychoanalytically and deconstructively about the transformations of human experience that are inevitable given our immersion in an accelerated hyper-technological environment is illustrated with a brief clinical example.

Chapter 4 then proceeds by introducing Derrida's account of *pharmaka* as that which function as both poison and remedy, and as that concept which forms the basis for Derrida's revolutionary thinking about the relationship between the human and the technological. This is in order to show how this way of thinking already structures Freud's comments on technology, as has been indicated in the critical project of the contemporary French philosopher Bernard Stiegler, who is arguably the most important philosopher working in the tradition of deconstruction today. Stiegler's voluminous publications offer opportunities for thinking the relationship between analytic practice and deconstruction in ways that insist on why these two projects remain irreducible for inventing a sustainable future far beyond either the academy or the clinic. Stiegler's account of the role of *technics* in the constitution of an attentive, symbolizing attitude allows for a rethinking of the meaning of clinical "technique" that discloses the proximity of psychoanalysis to the Heideggerian project for a fundamental ontology—a forerunner of Derridean deconstruction. Returning to Winnicott and to questions about how best to conceive the mother-infant relationship, I demonstrate how Stiegler, whose approach can be further integrated with clinical concerns, offers psychoanalysis a way to equip itself for facing the challenges of the now flooded global marketplace of therapeutic techniques.

I am inclined to anticipate that clinicians coming across a book on psychoanalysis and deconstruction are likely to be seized immediately by a good deal of skepticism. Perhaps even that expectation is too naively optimistic. My intention here is not merely to introduce deconstruction to a psychoanalytic audience. Such an effort could only wind up preaching to the converted, of which there must certainly be very few. What I wish to demonstrate are rather the ways in which certain concepts and experiences with which analysts are already intimately familiar—concepts and experiences that inform the specificity of psychoanalysis as a clinical practice, but that are for this very reason often the most difficult for analysts to articulate theoretically—have been elucidated by Derrida and other authors by whom he was influenced and by those who he influenced in turn. Despite its reputation as abstruse theory, the conceptual vocabulary and logic of deconstruction provides psychoanalysis with a means by which to clarify some of its more counterintuitive yet essential clinical insights and procedures.

I imagine that, should this book find an audience, it will be among academics with an interest in psychoanalytic theory. As a practicing analyst, however, I am writing in the hope of contacting my fellow clinicians, many of whom work every day with an acute sense of the crisis of the professional field. If they can put aside the understandable presumption that deconstruction is just a form of intellectual abstraction, and open themselves up to the hard work of grappling with texts that their training has not prepared them to consider seriously, I strongly believe that analysts will find in deconstruction a powerful resource for thinking about what is so unique to psychoanalysis as a form of therapeutic practice.

That said, I will not confine myself to a discussion of purely clinical concerns. Like Hegel, Marx, Nietzsche, Freud and Heidegger before him, Derrida was always interested in those moments when the ordinary opposition between theory and practice breaks down—that is, those moments when *thinking* creates *change*. This is why, despite having rarely commented on the experience of the psychoanalytic clinic, Derrida in fact has a great deal to say to those engaged in clinical practice. At the same time, this is also what makes deconstruction more than a merely theoretical or quasi-literary practice, and it is what opens deconstruction up to the practical dimensions of critical politics.

**10** Introduction

One of the arguments that I will repeatedly come back to and that will be fully developed in the last chapter concerns a way of thinking about psychoanalysis as a form of resistance to the destructive politics of global consumerism. This has nothing to do with situating psychoanalysis either on the left or on the right, or with judging the strength of its commitments either way. It does, however, have to do with distancing psychoanalysis from what has taken shape today in the form of the "mental health industry." I am aware that this might upset some readers who are close to or who are quick to identify with this industry, but my intention here is not simply polemical. The fate of psychoanalysis within such an industrial institution or network of institutions (bureaucratic, academic, pharmaceutical and so on)—each regulated by the demands of instrumental performance and of economic efficiency—is certain death. This is because industrialization inherently ruins the intimacy on which the practice of psychoanalysis is predicated. The moment that administrators begin to oversee an analytic process, or the moment an analysand is reduced to being a consumer of psychodynamic services, any therapeutic possibility is intrinsically corrupted. My deepest and most abiding sentiment with regard to the profession is that if psychoanalysis is to secure a place for itself in the twenty-first century it will have to be as a site of respite from and resistance to the often suicidal demands of the world in which we and our patients currently live.

## Notes

1 Largely thanks to Žižek's influence, English-speaking popular audiences still predisposed to an interest in "French philosophy" have for the most part declared deconstruction hopelessly out of fashion. Today these mass audiences have retreated into a position of being captivated by Lacan, who they had previously denounced based largely on a misguided reading of Derrida's criticisms of a few Lacanian texts, having ignored the fact that Derrida was always more appreciative than critical of Lacan. Peterson, who does not merit serious attention as an intellectual but whose powerful reach into contemporary reactionary politics should not be underestimated, has declared Derrida to be the most dangerous among "the postmodernists" (a nebulous Red conspiracy that he relentlessly reviles) and an avatar of cultural psychosis who was "pathological to the core" (Peterson 2017). Like most who denounce Derrida's name, Peterson makes such claims while simultaneously admitting that he finds Derrida's texts incomprehensible.

2 Again in conversation with Roudinesco, Derrida stated, "I have always mistrusted the cult of the identitarian, as well as that of the communitarian discourse often associated with it. I am seeking to recall the more and more necessary dissociation between the political and the territorial. So I share your anxiety concerning the communitarian logic, the identitarian compulsion, and like you I resist this movement that tends toward a narcissism of minorities that is developing everywhere—including within feminist movements" (2004, p. 21; see also pp. 25–32).

3 In his contribution to a volume celebrating Gill's influence on American psychoanalysis, Irwin Hoffman wrote, "The organizing principle that Gill believed should replace Freud's basic concept of energy discharge is 'the person point of view.' For Gill, the term person connotes both the *agency* of the subject of analytic investigation and treatment and the subject's *social* nature" (Silverman and Wolitzky 2013, p. 62; emphases in original). What

is interesting to note here is that Gill is remembered as an important figure in the history of ego psychology, which in American analytic circles is often known as "one person psychology," in contrast to the "two person psychology" of American interpersonalism. Interpersonal and "relational" psychoanalysts often distinguish themselves from a "classical Freudian" approach by insisting that it is their consideration of the dignity of subjective agency and of the social context in which such agency articulates itself that sets them apart from a traditionally biologistic approach. Gill's writings make it very clear that the intersubjective "two person" model is not a form of resistance to, but the logical extension of, a "one person" egological model. Beyond the limitations of Freud's occasional use of pneumatological metaphors, what Gill and his followers were attempting to remove from psychoanalytic history was an image of the psyche as an apparatus, a machine, in favor of a return to the humanist, moral ideal of the "person" as the subject of absolute freedom. This was because it has been difficult for analysts to imagine a machine that is not thoroughly deterministic, which is precisely what Derrida invites us to consider, and in such a way that could potentially put the tired and divisive debates between "one person" and "two person" psychologies finally to rest.

## References

Bleger, J. (1967) "Psycho-Analysis of the Psycho-Analytic Frame." *International Journal of Psycho-Analysis*. Pp. 511–519.

Derrida, J. (1978). *Writing and Difference*. Trans. A. Bass. Chicago, IL: University of Chicago Press.

Derrida, J. (1981). *Dissemination*. Trans. B. Johnson. Chicago, IL: University of Chicago Press.

Derrida, J. (1987). *The Post Card: From Socrates to Freud and Beyond*. Trans. A. Bass. Chicago, IL: University of Chicago Press.

Derrida, J. (1987). *The Truth in Painting*. Trans. G. Bennington and I. Mcleod. Chicago, IL: University of Chicago Press.

Derrida, J. (1990). *Glas*. Trans. John P. Leavey and Richard Rand. Lincoln, NE: University of Nebraska Press.

Derrida, J. (2007). "Telepathy." In: *Psyche: Inventions of the Other, Volume 1*. Ed. Peggy Kamuf and Elizabeth Rottenberg. Stanford, CA: Stanford University Press. Pp. 226–261.

Derrida, J., & Roudinesco, E. (2004). *For What Tomorrow…* Trans. J. Fort. Stanford, CA: Stanford University Press.

Dick, K., & Ziering, A., Dirs. (2002). *Derrida*.

Ferry, L., & Renaut, A. (1990). *French Philosophy of the Sixties: An Essay on Antihumanism*. Trans. M. Cattani. Amherst, MA: University of Massachusetts Press.

Freud, S. (1930). *Civilization and Its Discontents*. S.E. 21: pp. 57–146.

Hoffman, I. (2013). "Merton M. Gill: A Study in Theory Development in Psychoanalysis." In Silverman, D. and Wolitzky, D., Eds.: *Changing Conceptions of Psychoanalysis: The Legacy of Merton M. Gill*. New York: Routledge.

Peterson, J. (2017). www.youtube.com/watch?v=FTxmKc80wUw. Retrieved 5.10.17.

Silverman, D., & Wolitzky, D., Eds. (2013). *Changing Conceptions of Psychoanalysis: The Legacy of Merton M. Gill*. New York: Routledge.

# 1
# DIFFERANCE AND PSYCHIC SPACE

In what should be considered a classic text of the psychoanalytic literature, *The Matrix of the Mind*, Thomas Ogden (1986) quotes a patient who tells him,

> There is me and there is something inside me, not something, but someone, but since that someone is inside me, I can have an idea of who it is and not just be it. Sometimes this is connected with a feeling that it's a physical space inside my body, but it's sometimes in my head or isn't located any specific place in my body. It's a feeling, not a place, but it feels like a place.
>
> (p. 128)

This is an enviable example of the kind of clinical insight to which all analysts aspire. The patient raises questions about what it means to be a "me" (a subject) with an "inside" (a mind) as a "someone" (an individual) inhabited by a "something" (an other). The difference between the patient's sense of identity (the "me" that is a "someone") and of difference (the "something" that is an "inside") is mediated by an "idea" that differs from or that defers her simply *being* this other, which would involve a betrayal of herself. Thanks to the work of analysis, *thinking* inserts itself between the patient and who she *is*—how she thinks and behaves, which has since become other than and is no longer equivalent to her sense of self. This experience is not static and pre-determined: *sometimes* it feels different than at other times, and in ways that are experienced as having to do with what it's like to be inside a body or to be a body with an inside, which is *sometimes* different from what it feels like to "have" a mind or to be "in" her head. It is a feeling that is also a place, but not necessarily a place that is "in" the body or "in" the mind. The feeling is that this is a place, but there is also an idea that it is something other than or different from a place. It is difficult for the patient to describe exactly what it is that she is feeling or experiencing because what is at issue is the relationship between feeling,

**14** Difference and psychic space

thinking and experiencing. This difficulty is not an impasse—to the contrary, it is a moment of integration and of forward momentum in the treatment, even though it is not clear to the patient or to the analyst what exactly it is that she is working to describe. The patient is putting into words the very primitive sense that she can be different from who or what or from the way she ordinarily is—that she is open to other possibilities and to the possibility of otherness. This is what psychoanalysis is all about.

Everyday clinical moments are not always this potent, but they do often contain reference to an ongoing process of development and change through space and over time, even when this is not readily apparent. The twists and turns of the clinical narrative depict the contours of psychological space as this is elaborated and as it evolves: the patient is talking about her boyfriend; suddenly she "has a thought" or "finds herself" thinking of an incident she had witnessed in her parents' relationship. What links these two thoughts is a space whose dynamically evolving interior can then be fleshed out and filled with associative understanding. By means of this spatializing process, new perspectives can be opened up and new positions in relation to what was previously considered unquestionable reality can be assumed. The owning and integration of these possibilities from which inner experience can be reflected upon are the goals of an insight-oriented approach to treatment. In order to accomplish this, psychoanalysis offers the patient the opportunity to refine the capacity for symbolizing his or her experience, so that the boundaries of agency are expanded—so that I (as a symbolizing subject) might come to be in the place where "it" (unsymbolized experience, to which one feels passively subjected) resides.

At the same time, the therapeutic process must also be understood as a process of temporalization. Telling stories takes time. Narration and transference open up and unfold over the course of the treatment. Symbolization occurs when the patient's stories begin to reveal to him the interaction of past, present and future. The question governing interpretation of the transference is always: What is the contemporary relevance of the story the patient is elaborating? Why is he telling *this* particular story *now*? The very act of selecting and telling stories comes to have meaning, and the unfolding of narratives of the past is understood as significant in its function of representing the present. We understand that in the present we repeat and therefore we symbolically represent our past through our symptoms, interpersonal failures, actings out, etc. What is always more elusive is how, in the act of recounting the past, we represent the present. How is the telling of stories of the past a determining factor in the experience of the present? In treatment, we tell our presents by recounting our pasts. This is why an insight-oriented clinical approach produces a therapeutic effect: to *re*-present the present is to *repeat difference*—to allow for the possibility of change. To allow for the possibility of change is to become differentiated: to become oneself in allowing oneself to become other than oneself. This is intrinsic to what is meant by symbolization.

The development of symbolizing capacities promotes enhanced reflection on the complexities of experience. It is worth rehearsing the fact that the concept of reflection itself contains both spatial and temporal dimensions: it implies a certain distance between consciousness and the object of contemplation as poles between which reflection occurs, as well as the repetition of a previous encounter between the two (*reflection*). Over the time of reflection, the space of reflection opens; in the space of reflection, the time of reflection unfolds. Consciousness, as the experience of the self reflecting itself into itself in ways that can potentially cultivate openness and transformation, might best be understood in relation to this space and this time.

Despite the crucial interplay of spatial and temporal metaphors in both psychoanalytic theory and psychoanalytic practice, spatial metaphors historically have been granted the upper hand. Until relatively recently, time has not been a subject of great attention for British and American analysts, with Loewald (1962, 1972) and Winnicott (1971) being notable exceptions. Even today, the concept of psychic or inner space always implicates a notion of time in a way that remains generally unthought. Distinguishing between the subjectively internal and the objectively external has traditionally depended upon space as a metaphor for comparing the two. It is certainly not an accident that the familiar conceptualization of subjective interiority appeals to space instead of to time in this sense. To contemplate "inner time" would require an effort to think an outside that inheres within time itself. This is not a familiar concept; it is, however, a concept—or rather an effort to think something that remains unfamiliar to the extent that it tests the limits of ordinary conceptual understanding—at the very heart of the project of deconstruction.

As a critique of the general organization of the Western tradition as a "metaphysics of presence"—an uncritical valorization of the present *now* and of self-presence or self-identity as the model for thinking the essential natures of mind and world—deconstruction, and Derrida's work in particular, provides the resources for an attempt to consider the representative functions of space and time in any effort to outline a scientific approach to the study of mind—that is, an approach that addresses and is therefore not determined by its own tendencies toward idealism and metaphysics. Carried out to its most rigorous and exacting limits, this effort would also allow for a consideration of the loss in representation that these functions necessarily involve—that is, the extent to which mind as thoughtful self-reflection cannot be all-encompassing but must always generate some remainder of unthought difference.

Since the serious study of mind is a complex and sophisticated effort, a complex and sophisticated theoretical approach is warranted. This does not mean that we should lose sight of the at least formal simplicity of the questions to be addressed: To what are we referring when we use the concept of psychic or inner space? How do we account for the intuitive coherence of such a concept, and why does a complementary concept of "inner time" not similarly and readily recommend itself? What are the implications of thinking inner experience in terms of space, what opportunities are opened up to and which are closed down? Perhaps thinking about individual experience in terms of psychic or inner space limits what can be experienced as internal, and to the extent that a sense of the internal is already a spatially determined articulation of our experience. In that case, are there other ways of thinking about psychic reality that the concept of psychic

**16** Difference and psychic space

space leaves inaccessible? These are very general questions that cannot be treated in their entirety. My concern is with the way one might open these questions, and to do so will require an attempt to think rigorously and precisely the sense of their "opening." To borrow from Derrida (1978, p. 199) a way of stating the problem: We are not asking what is psychic space, but what is space, and what is the psyche if it can be represented by space?

## Psychic space and the mother-infant

Examining the history of spatial metaphors in psychoanalytic thinking since Freud would be a potentially interminable project. Very complex treatments of space as an interior dimension are already present in Freud's earliest reflections on the psyche. However, while Freud's writings certainly reflect a spatialized sense of the unconscious—the "contents" of which were to be the object of the new "depth psychology"—it was with Melanie Klein's work that a more definitively spatialized rendition of mental life was realized. Moving away from the temporal dimension implied by the concept of unconscious memory, Klein's focus on the impact of internal objects implicitly described the psyche as a spatial environment by establishing a symmetry between introjection and projection. Whereas Ferenczi (1913) had earlier described introjection as an expansion of ego boundaries rather than as an induction of psychic material, Klein thought introjection as the installation of object-phantasies "within" the mind, and projection as their removal "outside" the mind. While a spatial understanding of mind was not explicitly argued for, by casting both development and psychopathology in terms of the vicissitudes of introjection and projection, Klein invented an entire tradition of thinking about psychic processes in spatially absolute terms.

Winnicott was the first to attempt an understanding of the origins and development of psychic space explicitly conceived of as such. In order to understand how an individuated psyche might come into existence through its interactions with an already constituted parental psyche, Winnicott introduced the concept of a potential or transitional space. It is this transitional space that facilitates the mother's adoption of her infant as her own, and that cultivates in the developing child the sense that there is a world at large worth connecting up to and investing in. The theory of transitional phenomena attempts to situate shared experience within a thinking that is not governed by a classical subject/object logic or framework.

"Transitional Objects and Transitional Phenomena" is the pivot around which much of Winnicott's most important work turns. *Playing and Reality* (1971) is a return to and an expansion of the themes initially laid out there. Here Winnicott offers a meditation on the difficulties inherent in attempting to grasp the concept of potential space and its relation to our familiar understanding of the absolute division between subjective and objective experience. Over and over again, Winnicott struggles to convey the sense of potential space as a concept that exceeds our familiar way of conceiving the split between inner and outer reality, individual and other.

The interactive engagement of spatial and temporal metaphors throughout the book approximates another central concept Winnicott develops: playing. Playing is a word that Winnicott appropriates from everyday language and makes thoroughly his own, yet this is something that his readers often seem not fully to have grasped. At times it is space that is grasped as the crucial point of reference for the exposition of this concept, and in other places it is time. In virtually every case where the one is privileged, the other emerges in turn to capture what is being lost:

> I make my idea of play concrete by claiming that *playing has a place* and a time. It is not *inside* by any use of the word (and it is unfortunately true that the word inside has very many and various uses in psychoanalytic discussion). Nor is it *outside*, that is to say, it is not part of the repudiated world, the not-me, that which the individual has decided to recognize (with whatever difficulty and even pain) as truly external, which is outside magical control. To control what is outside one has to *do* things, not simply think or wish, and *doing things takes time*. Playing is doing.
>
> (Winnicott 1971, p. 41; emphases in original)

Winnicott chooses to italicize and insist on the idea that "*playing has a place.*" There is a place of play, a space in which—or as which—the activity of playing transpires. The idea that playing has a time is not similarly italicized. In attempting to describe this space of playing, Winnicott concedes that it cannot be thought with reference to an understanding of the (adult) distinction between inside and outside. In order to think the idea that "*playing has a place*"—a place that resists our thinking of space as coordinated in relation to the opposition between inside and outside—Winnicott appeals to the experience of time. Because playing occurs in a place that is neither inside nor outside our experience of space, because it extends beyond our experience of space as determined by the opposition of the inside and the outside, it can only be articulated with reference to time understood as an outside or as an other of space itself. The infant's transition from omnipotence fantasy to the recognition of a reality that can be tested requires that the infant "do things." And according to Winnicott, doing things in the *space* of playing takes *time*: "*doing things takes time.*" Here time is italicized and insisted upon. In the brief space of a single paragraph, Winnicott transitions from privileging space to privileging time in his attempt to articulate the site of playing. Later he writes:

> It is perhaps worth while trying to formulate this in a way that gives the time factor due weight. The feeling of the mother's existence lasts $x$ minutes. If the mother is away more than $x$ minutes, then the imago fades, and along with this the baby's capacity to use the symbol of the union ceases. The baby is distressed, but this distress is soon *mended* because the mother returns in $x + y$ minutes. In $x + y$ minutes the baby has not become altered. But in $x + y + z$ minutes the baby has become *traumatized*. [...F]rom the effects of $x + y + z$ degree of deprivation, babies are constantly being *cured* by the mother's localized spoiling that mends the ego structure. This mending of the

**18** Difference and psychic space

ego structure re-establishes the baby's capacity to use a symbol of union; the baby then comes once more to allow and even to benefit from separation. *This is the place that I have set out to examine*, the separation that is not a separation but a form of union.

(1971, pp. 97–98; emphases in original)

Here Winnicott attempts to give time its due in thinking about shared experience. The continuity of the baby's experience is constantly under a barrage of breakages as the mother appears and disappears within the perceptual field. The mother's presence effects a mending of ego structure if it occurs following a brief period of absence. Following a longer period of absence the baby is traumatized and the capacity to use physical interaction as a symbol of unity is lost. The mother's reappearance, to the extent that it is reinforced by "localized spoiling," reestablishes the baby's ability to use their interaction as a symbol through which the illusion of union can be maintained and separation can be gradually negotiated. The interplay between continuity and discontinuity in the infant's experience is dependent upon the mother's behavior as it contrasts with the infant's fantasies of omnipotence. The timing of the difference between moments of continuity and discontinuity can be traumatic, but the mother's ability to repair the ego can allow the baby to use this timing in the service of separation. The difference between temporal continuity and discontinuity is thereby itself enlisted in the symbolization of experience. The organization of this difference is the "outside" of the experiences of temporal continuity and discontinuity that functions to sustain the infant's fragile psyche over time. Winnicott calls this the "*place*" with which his thinking is concerned.

Winnicott's developmental schema traces the emergence of potential or transitional space in the mother-infant matrix, by way of which the mother and the infant are able to emerge as fully differentiated beings. In a Winnicottian vein, Ogden (1986) writes, "The study of psychological development is not simply the study of the growth of the infantile psyche from primitivity to maturity; it is also the study of the development of the mother-infant into a mother and infant" (p. 172). The development of the mother and infant dyad out of the mother-infant unity depends on the mother's ability both to protect the infant from, and simultaneously to introduce him to, reality as separation and difference. In advancing the theme of a potential or transitional region of experience, Ogden outlines how the concepts of the mother-and-infant dyad and the mother-infant unity are no longer tenable, or rather tend toward extreme displacements once the concept of potential or transitional space is introduced. Transitional space names the negotiation of the differences between the mother-infant unit of primary narcissism and the mother and infant as they come to be known as separate individuals. As a reflection on this transitional region between unity and difference, Winnicott's thinking explores not this latter difference, but rather the difference between unity and difference determined in opposition to unity as separation ("the separation that is not a separation but a form of union"). The concept of transitional space therefore describes a transitive difference between self and other more complex than the absolute difference between self and other that has been the object of classical thought. The concepts of the mother-infant unity and of the mother and infant dyad are in turn revealed as provisional, describing structures of experience possible only after transitional objects have intervened in the developmental process (Winnicott 1960, p. 39). In order to understand the mother-infant relationship—which is not a relationship between subjects and objects in a classical sense—and its development into the mother and infant as separate beings then, new ways of thinking are required (Winnicott 1971, p. 14; Ogden 1986, p. 182).

While it is therefore strictly incorrect to speak of mother *and* infant at birth, it is equally incorrect to speak of the mother-infant as a purely homogenous field. Despite the fact that the mother and infant have yet to become differentiated, this does not mean that their original "unity" can be considered an undifferentiated matrix: "Since the mother-infant is a psychological entity contributed to by (what an outside observer would designate as) the mother and the infant, the unit of psychological development is always both a primitive psychological organization and a relatively mature one" (Ogden 1986, p. 173). There is a subtle tautology here that continues to impose itself and with which Ogden struggles: one has to make reference to the mother and the infant as separate in order to describe the original mother-infant relationship; yet it is from the vantage point of the dyadic mother and infant model that the mother-infant is inappropriately described as a homogenous "unity." Only if we select the mother and infant relationship as a privileged point of reference—which we are in fact constrained to do—does the mother-infant relationship appear as an undifferentiated field.

The idea of the mother-infant as neither a site of singular oneness, nor a classical interaction between two separate beings, suggests a picture of development in which differences that do not yet refer back to differentiated subjects or objects interact with one another to bring about the mother and the infant as psychically distinct individuals. It is only in relation to this later developmental achievement that it seems appropriate to refer to their original state as oneness. By privileging the infant's development into an adult subject as the model of effective individuation, the original mother-infant relationship cannot appear as anything but a state of total non-differentiation, in which the infant recognizes no difference between itself and its environment. Non-differentiation, however, fails to describe the fact that "the unit of psychological development is always *both a primitive psychological organization and a relatively mature one*"—which is to say that it is neither a unit nor an interaction classically conceived, but must be thought otherwise beyond the limits of this opposition. The mother-infant relationship might then be conceptualized rather as an intersection of "pure differences"—a term that must be put under quotation marks in order to underscore its provisional character—from which the mother and the infant eventually emerge as separate entities.

The "pure differences" which compose the mother-infant matrix may be thought of as progressively organized around the axes of age, gender and sexuality. These differences are not "pure" because they are real with respect to the mother's adult identity, but on the contrary because the traces of the mother's own

**20** Difference and psychic space

developmental sequence are activated throughout child-rearing. What interacts within the mother-infant matrix is not the mother and the infant as they come to be determined as separate individuals following on the process of developmental differentiation; rather, it is the differences between what will only later emerge in the organized forms of mother and infant that are active-passively interacting. Moreover, it should be insisted again that despite a certain rhetorical convenience, it is not that these differences interact "within" the mother-infant matrix; these differences-in-interaction *are* the mother-infant matrix as the *space* of their differentiation *over time*. The difficulties inherent in elaborating this idea—an idea that is nonetheless lodged deep at the heart of writings by Winnicott, Ogden and other like-minded theorists in the field—lead Ogden to state:

> Because the internal holding environment of the infant, his own psychological matrix, takes *time* to develop, the infant's mental contents initially exist within the matrix of the maternal mental and physical activity. In other words, in the beginning, the environmental mother provides the *mental space* in which the infant begins to generate experience. It is in this sense that I believe a new psychological entity is created by the mother and (what is becoming) the infant.
>
> (1986, p. 180; emphases added)

Ogden here repeats precisely the gesture noted earlier in Winnicott's work: reflection on the function of time in the interaction between mother and infant leads inevitably to a theory of the genesis of mental space.

Like Winnicott, Ogden does not attempt specifically to theorize this conceptual slippage. The clinical relevance of doing so is apparent in his treatment of symbolization. Working for the most part from a contemporary Kleinian perspective, Ogden situates the development of subjectivity in the transition from the paranoid-schizoid position to the depressive position. More specifically, subjectivity is forged in the emergence of the capacity for symbolization from dependence on symbolic equation. Symbolization is understood here as the ability to give meaning to one's perceptions and to acknowledge reality as cognitively mediated; symbolic equation is the refutation of the difference between perception and reality (Segal 1957). It is in the opening of a "space" between symbol and symbolized that the ability to interpret and to own one's experience is made possible. Prior to the opening of the difference between symbol and symbolized—between subjective interpretation and objective world—there is no sense of agency, but rather a diffuse sense of events that simply happen. This experience is retreated to defensively through splitting: "The mental operation of splitting creates a state of mind in which there is 'no in between'" (Ogden 1986, p. 62).

When splitting predominates to such an extent that "there is no psychological vantage point from which more than one emotional plane can be taken in," the effect is that, "History is instantaneously rewritten" (p. 62). As Ogden vividly describes, momentary anger and disappointment with the analyst provokes the borderline patient to disavow all other, previous experiences of the analyst which do not accord with his immediate perception: "the patient simply does not remember feeling other than he does at present" (p. 62). While involved in such a state these patients cannot see that their experience of the analyst while angry or disappointed reflects those feeling states; instead, it is as if the reality of the analyst's malevolence has been finally unveiled. The space in which the patient normally mediates between the symbol (the immediate experience of the analyst colored by anger) and the symbolized (the analyst as a person who has affected the patient in several different affectively-determined guises over the course of the transference) is collapsed.

What is important to recognize here is that the collapse of internal *space* produces a *temporal* effect. The reduction of the space between symbol and symbolized proceeds by way of "an assault on the history of the object relationship. The present is projected backward and forward, thus creating a static, eternal, nonreflective present" (p. 62). Since the space between the symbol and the symbolized is also the time of their historicized relationship, the collapse of psychic space proceeds by way of an obliteration of psychic time. Tracing the contours of this obliteration brings us to the import of Derrida's thinking.

## Spacing and differance

Despite its reputation, deconstruction is not, nor was it ever, a philosophy of language. Derrida's early analysis of the concept of the sign proved itself neither limited nor dedicated to a purely linguistic concern. A critical approach to the concept of the sign was exemplary in a particular historical and intellectual context as a means by which to launch a much larger and more powerful project. Against Saussure's (1959) understanding of the relationship between signifier and signified as arbitrary, Derrida observed rather that this relationship cannot be arbitrary, though it cannot be said to conform to a determinable causal logic either. In *Of Grammatology* (1976) Derrida argued that the priority Saussure grants to the sign, rather than securing a scientific foundation for linguistics, instead threatens the very idea of language as it has been traditionally understood. Once the signifier is considered radically independent of that which it is said to represent, or once its relation to a preceding instance of meaning which it is supposed to relay is deemed arbitrary, the definition of language as a vehicle designed to communicate subjective intention is undermined. The relationship between signifier and signified can therefore be neither arbitrary nor calculable if language is to remain a meaningful concept. The opposition of the material (signifier) and the ideal (signified) expressed by the concept of the sign must be reconsidered.

This reflection on the sign as neither coherently determinable nor chaotically arbitrary opened up to a more general thinking of an outside of classical logic that is not its simple opposite (i.e. contradiction, nonsense or madness). As Derrida repeatedly demonstrated across his texts, arbitrariness always involves a certain kind of determinacy, and determinacy always involves a certain kind of arbitrariness. What

**22** Difference and psychic space

is at play between the two, as between the figures in any conventional opposition, is the neither active nor passive operation of what Derrida termed differance.

This word has caused a considerable amount of confusion in the history of the reception of Derrida's work, particularly in the United States where deconstruction was too quickly taken up by and associated with university departments of comparative literature and cultural studies. To help ease the effects of this confusion, I will not leave the word untranslated (as *différance*) because this encourages the English-speaking reader momentarily to adopt a phony French accent which doubly betrays Derrida's intention by making the difference between "difference" and "differance" something audible rather than something graphic (1982, pp. 3–5), and by making the word to appear—and more importantly, to function, as again the history of the reception of Derrida's work in the United States amply makes clear— as a master signifier that seems capable of governing a given discourse. "Differance" should be heard homonymously with "difference." Paradoxically, leaving the word untranslated has the effect of concealing its meaning in its original idiom, which is the opposite intention of any decision to remain faithful to the original by leaving a term untranslated within an otherwise translated text. It is this very paradoxical and self-othering, differing/deferring logic that Derrida aimed to elucidate, without ever claiming to be fully capable of pinning it down.

The neologism differance (which in the original French is not entirely a neologism) attempts to introduce a thinking of the idea of difference which does not submit itself to the values historically ascribed to the concepts of the singular, the whole, the identical, and the One. This was a project called for by Heidegger at "the end of philosophy" (1972), in which "the matter of thinking is the difference *as* difference" (1969, p. 47; emphasis in original). As the substantive form of the French verb *différer* (to defer), differance suspends any determination of its status as either active or passive, and as either a noun or a verb, opening up to a consideration of how a concept might differ from itself, in this case meaning both to differ and to defer. This is not an instance of polysemy but a deferral of any ultimate, final meaning, even multiple meanings. The *a* of differance—which cannot be heard, which is silent or absent except in what is written—is indicative of the fact that the word does not intend to refer to anything, it does not attempt to give a name to an object of positive cognition. In differing from itself, and in thereby lacking any singular, specifiable meaning, differance rather attempts to account for what makes cognition possible while withdrawing itself from circulation. As a consequence, Derrida demonstrates, differance cannot be considered fundamental, it cannot be a ground or center from which a new philosophical system or method might derive. Quite the contrary, differance "prevents any word, any concept, any major enunciation from coming to summarize and to govern from the theological presence of a center the movement [...] of differences" (Derrida 1981, p. 14). Differance therefore describes "the systematic play of differences, of the traces of differences, of the *spacing* by means of which elements are related to each other. This spacing is the simultaneously active and passive [...] production of the intervals without which the 'full' terms would not signify, would not function" (p. 27); it designates the manner in which the terms of any relationship are originally related to themselves, the erasure of which relates these terms to one another in the form of an apparent exteriority as opposition.

Bringing together the senses of differentiation and deferral, and relating the one to the other reciprocally in terms of differentiation and deferral, Derrida's difference offers a way of treating the relationship between the terms in any conceptual hierarchy as non-static, reversible and modifiable with respect to a certain critical rigor. In order to apply this rigor to the concept of psychic space as outlined in the previous section, it is instructive first to rehearse Derrida's early writings on the relationship between consciousness and the voice as the repression of difference constitutive of Western thought as a metaphysics of presence.

In *Speech and Phenomena* (1973) and *Of Grammatology* (1976), Derrida analyzed the structure of conscious experience as self-relation in the form of "hearing-oneself-speak." When I speak I also hear myself speaking, and generally in such way that makes these two gestures appear perfectly synchronous. For Derrida, it is in the event of hearing-oneself-speak that consciousness is determined as the form of self experience in general: "What is said of sound in general is a fortiori valid for the *phonē* by which, by virtue of hearing (understanding)-oneself-speak—an indissociable system—the subject affects itself and is related to itself in the element of ideality" (1976, p. 12). Hearing-oneself-speak produces an ideal proximity of the signifier and the signified—an apparent identity between those sounds I use to express myself and what meaning it is that I wish to express.

In using my body to make sounds that are sent out into the world for the purpose of communicating meaning, these sounds return to my body in the immediacy of my hearing-myself-speak, creating a circuit between what I say and what I mean that reduces the difference between the two. The effect of this proximity-as-reduction is that it appears that I know and intend what I want to say before I say it, and that when I say it, it is immediately identical to itself as what I meant internally before it was produced vocally and put forth into the world. The total effect of this phonic circuit of self-reference is to conceive of consciousness as an origin of meaning and as possessed of an intention to communicate itself: "The voice is the being which is present to itself in the form of universality, as consciousness; the voice *is* consciousness" (1973, pp. 79–80; emphasis in original). The "indissociable system" of hearing-oneself-speak as the production of consciousness as self-presence accounts for the "strange privilege of sound in idealization" (1976, p. 12) that Derrida diagnosed in his early readings of Husserl's phenomenology and Saussure's linguistics.

This was a deconstructive account of the experience of consciousness as self-consciousness—as an effect of the illusory sense of immediacy produced by an act of reduction, in which the voice obscures its own passage of becoming. Hearing-oneself-speak effaces or "forgets" the passage of the voice from the mouth to the ears:

**24** Difference and psychic space

> When I speak, not only am I conscious of being present for what I think, but I am conscious also of keeping as close as possible to my thought, or to the "concept," a signifier that does not fall into the world, a signifier that I hear as soon as I emit it, that seems to depend upon my pure and free spontaneity, requiring the use of no instrument, no accessory, no force taken from the world. Not only do the signifier and the signified seem to unite, but also, in this confusion, the signifier seems to erase itself or to become transparent, in order to allow the concept to present itself as what it is, referring to nothing other than its presence. The exteriority of the signifier is reduced.
>
> (Derrida 1981, p. 22)

In the passage of speech from the inside to the outside and back again in the event of hearing-oneself-speak, the interval of this passage which constitutes a self-*relation* is overtaken by the effect it subsequently produces—the effect of self as whole or identical to itself in the immediacy of its presence to itself. What is called self or consciousness here is understood as an *effect* of its relation *to itself*. In order to articulate this Derrida appeals to the phenomenological term "auto-affection"—a term mobilized largely by Heidegger but originally derived from Kant. Auto-affection names this self-relation or self-reference in such a way that marks the fact that this is a self-reference without a self, a kind of reference that produces an effect of self but which cannot therefore be termed "self-reference" or "self-reflection," since such a term presupposes a self existing prior to the event of its reflecting upon or referring to itself. Auto-affection means that there is no self prior to the event of self-reflection. To understand this we must think of self-reflection as something more than a merely psychological activity.

Auto-affection in the form of hearing-oneself-speak is an act of self-reference that produces self-identity, but towards which it cannot be said to be motivated except teleologically. This is why, for Derrida, "the voice *is* consciousness," and why the finite organic body or *trace*, as that which divides consciousness as self-presence from a past that it can appropriate only in the mode of a thoughtful reflection upon itself as embodied, is "indefinitely its own becoming-unmotivated" (1976, p. 47). Consciousness as self-consciousness requires a passage through the world in the form of the voice that is heard in order to be constituted as such; in this way the interior becomes interior only by means of a passage or sending through the exterior. In order for the interior to be itself, it must return to itself after a passage through that which is exterior to it, yet which only becomes exterior to it in turn. This is why, in Derrida's analysis of the structure of internal self-consciousness, the subjective interior and the objective, worldly exterior are not clearly demarcated, but must be understood as the ongoing, active-passive differentiation/deferral of one another.

If self-identity then, as consciousness produced by the voice in the circuit of hearing-oneself-speak, is to be understood as an effect without proper cause (as self-relation by which a self is effected), what is the object of the "unmotivated" reduction of the difference between speaking and hearing-oneself-speak in the

Difference and psychic space  **25**

movement that produces the self as self-proximity or self-presence? In *Speech and Phenomena*, Derrida writes:

> As pure auto-affection, the operation of hearing-oneself-speak seems to reduce even the inward surface of one's own body; in its phenomenal being it seems capable of dispensing with this exteriority within interiority, this interior space in which our experience or image of our own body is spread forth. This is why hearing-oneself-speak is experienced as an absolutely pure auto-affection, occurring in a self-proximity that would in fact be the absolute reduction of space in general.
>
> (1973, p. 79)

Anticipating the relationship here between his project and the Freudian concept of the unconscious (as a form of "exteriority within interiority"), while remaining fully within the academic discourse of phenomenology, Derrida is showing us how the commonsense, metaphysical idealization of consciousness is predicated on a hypostatization of time in the form of the absolute immediacy of the "now." Consciousness as self-proximity, or as the ideal proximity of signifier and signified in the event of hearing-oneself-speak, is here understood as the collapse of internal space—or rather, as the "absolute reduction of space in general," since it is the difference between the internal and the external that is under consideration. Hearing-oneself-speak creates an idealized sense of space and time that reduces or that "represses" its origin in a dissociation through which interior, psychological space is engendered. However, we cannot speak of dissociation in a conventional sense here as the splitting of a previously whole unity (i.e. the splitting of the ego). Properly speaking, nothing is actually split. What appears to be split (consciousness, the ego, the self) only appears *as* itself as an effect of this process of differentiation. Thus it is not that a dissociative split occurs in an originally undifferentiated or integrated field of self-experience; rather, self-experience emerges from a dissociation that dissociates "from itself" or without referent, as a kind of "pure reference" without object. This is what is meant by the movement of "an absolutely pure auto-affection," according to which inner or psychic space is understood as pre-existing a psyche or interior unit that can be treated as such. Psychic space therefore is not something that is created "in" the mind; the individual mind is an effect of the creation of psychic space, though it would seem to make no sense to speak of psychic space prior to the existence of an individual, differentiated psyche. For this reason, the psychiatric term "dissociation" fails to describe what is at issue here. What Derrida's work attempts to relate itself to is the dynamic opening of a space anterior to a field subject to any opening—an originary difference the thought of which is subject to a certain kind of reduction or repression.

Derrida's elusive rendition of inner space as an "exteriority within interiority" becomes more comprehensible (though no less challenging) in this regard. The logic of deconstruction argues that something must retain an essential relation to that which it absolutely is not in order for its identity to itself to be maintained.

**26** Difference and psychic space

For inner space to be inner space, it must constantly appeal to the external space from which it (actively-passively) differs. Furthermore, it must contain this perpetual reference to external space within itself as the form of its own self-relation. There would be no difference between inner and outer space—between me and not-me—if each did not at the same time differ from itself in order to contain the possibility of relating to the other. The terms of this differential relationship are formulated elsewhere in Derrida's work as *spacing*:

> An interval must separate the present from what it is not in order for the present to be itself, but this interval that constitutes it as present must, by the same token, divide the present in and of itself, thereby also dividing, along with the present, everything that is thought on the basis of the present, that is, in our metaphysical language, every being, and singularly substance or the subject. In constituting itself, in dividing itself dynamically, this interval is what might be called *spacing*, the becoming-time of space or the becoming-space of time (*temporization*).
>
> (1982, p. 13; emphases in original)

An interval must originally separate consciousness from itself in order for consciousness to emerge as self-reflection. Again, for Derrida, consciousness is the effect of this division, in that it cannot be said to precede it. Self-reflection emerges in a space that is "interior" to a generalized notion of recursive reflection itself.

Note that between the two passages just cited there appears the same tension or slippage between spatial and temporal metaphors evident in the work of Winnicott and Ogden: the object of consideration is contemplated at certain moments as a temporal interval, and at other moments as a spatial distance. The originality of Derrida's thinking lies in its attempt to formulate this slippage as an irreducible, dynamic movement inherent to all aspects of our theorizing, one that indicates a certain openness of thought. Derrida appeals directly to this tension—where at times it is appropriate to approach the object of consideration in terms of space, and at other times in terms of time—in order to demonstrate that this is not a problem with our attempt at conceptual coherence; rather it is a necessary condition governing all our attempts to render experience in conceptual, theoretical terms, and it can therefore be formalized and deployed strategically. Here this tension is organized conceptually as *spacing*. Spacing designates the inadequacy of both temporal and spatial conceptualizations of subjective experience (as the immediacy of self-presence or self-identity, or as the solipsistic boundedness of inner space) where the one is not continuously and actively related to the other. The intransitive form spa*cing* reminds us that this is also a temporal phenomenon, a temporalizing function, though it is never purely spatializing nor purely temporalizing.

In order to retain the sense of spacing both as a discrete concept and as a structure at work in the overall dynamic of Derrida's conceptual economy, spacing must be constantly related to other structures in Derrida's work such as supplement, trace, dissemination, and differ*ance*. None of these terms function as a conceptual ground

Difference and psychic space **27**

that would convert critical thought into a philosophical system. Thus whereas the intransitive spacing comprehends the irreducible co-implication of space and time in any consideration of psychic interiority, the non-transitive differance refigures the relationship between comprehension and irreducibility with respect to space and time as complementary limits of theory (i.e. consciousness) in general. What this means is that, whereas spacing is "the becoming-absent and the becoming-unconscious of the [conscious] subject" (1976, p. 69), differance as "neither a word nor a concept" (1982, p. 3) describes the relationship between the conscious and the unconscious, the inside and the outside, etc., such that the movement of becoming-absent, as an inescapable loss in representation inherent in any theoretical system, can retain its greatest effectiveness by being constantly (though never absolutely) accounted for and related to. In this way Derrida's thinking facilitates the deconstruction of the metaphysical opposition of theory and practice.

For any approach, either theoretical or clinical, to the unconscious and its place in inner and interpersonal experience, Derrida is calling here for a considerable reworking of our ordinary understanding of the relationships between consciousness, the unconscious and defense. What binds consciousness and the voice in the form of identity as self-presence is the repression of a kind of difference that inhabits the possibility of enunciation and that upsets any rigid opposition of mind and world. Freud formulates this difference as the unconscious: the possibility that something might mean something other than what the conscious speaking subject believes it is intended to mean, that something might speak "in" or *through* me yet that *is not* me. Where saying whatever comes to mind is the only rule imposed on the patient, and a neutral, interpretive stance is assumed by the analyst, treatment is a guided confrontation with this possibility in the context of hearing-oneself-speak.

Derrida draws on a Freudian register to develop a way of thinking differance while at the same time criticizing those elements of Freud's thought that resist the implications of its own discovery. Terms such as "primary repression," for instance, which attempt to account for the "origin" of an unconscious (Freud 1915), at the same time fall within the history of the idealization of time conceived of on the basis of consciousness as self-presence, which the concept of the unconscious does so much to deconstruct. Derrida appeals to a thinking outside this idealization by problematizing the concept of origin, allowing for a notion of the unconscious that is not determined by the model of a conscious subject originally present to itself. As concerns the notion of psychic space, this would require a temporalized and spatialized understanding of the unconscious, temporalized and spatialized according to a thinking of space and time that tries to account for a concept like the unconscious. In discussing such a project, Arkady Plotnitsky (1994) emphasizes that:

> Even as it produces the effects of consciousness and self-consciousness, differance irreducibly subtracts from the plenitude of consciousness or self-consciousness, individual or collective; or from the metaphysically conceived plenitude or presence of the unconscious. The unconscious cannot in turn

**28** Differance and psychic space

> be thought of as existing by itself, in the fullness of its presence, absolutely
> outside consciousness or in metaphysical opposition to it.
>
> (pp. 56–57)

It is in recasting the way that the unconscious is thought in terms of an absolute
difference to consciousness—by thinking their relation rather in terms of differentiation and deferral—that Derrida's work finds its clinical applicability: "*Strategically*,
Derrida's deconstruction employs an opposition between consciousness and the
unconscious" (Plotnitsky 1994, p. 57; emphasis added). Psychoanalysis uses this
opposition strategically as well in its clinical application, despite the fact that Freud
provided us with the "metaphysical name of the unconscious" (Derrida 1982, p. 20).
Derrida's approach, however, does not simply insist on a more dynamic or radical
sense of the concept of the unconscious; rather it rewrites the relationship between
consciousness and unconsciousness as dimensions of subjective experience, and in
such a way that destabilizes any absolute opposition between the *intra*subjective and
the *inter*subjective. It is for this reason that deconstruction, as has often been noted,
bears a closer resemblance to the practice than to the theories of psychoanalysis.

## Psyche as space and treatment as play

The economy of differance attempts to comprehend, among other things, the relationship between spatial and temporal frameworks in the effort to portray subjective experience in its commerce with external, objective reality. Articulating the
relationship between space and time in terms that are not derived from the metaphysical framework that opposes the subjective and the objective upends the foundational authority of that opposition. Conceiving of inner experience as psychic
space, and of reality as the space of the external world requires the deployment of
temporal metaphors as a means by which to stage the relationship between the two.
The appeal of differance to differentiation—its spatial side, so to speak—is unthinkable without recourse to its sense of temporality as deferral and delay. Differance
therefore involves a meditation on the meaning of the concept of difference as the
movement of its own displacement—the way in which the concept of difference
differs from and defers itself, without which the word difference would not name
difference but a form of identity. This meditation is in itself (temporally) interminable and (spatially) uncontainable, hence the necessity of relating its operation to
the effects of other concepts such as trace, supplement, dissemination and writing,
as well as space, force, sign and the unconscious.

Exploring the meaning of difference in terms of (spatial) differentiation pushes
into the foreground its sense as a process that occurs over time. Thus, according
to Derrida, "*Différer* in this sense is to temporize, to take recourse, consciously
or unconsciously, in the temporal and temporizing mediation of a detour that
suspends the accomplishment or fulfillment of 'desire' or 'will,' and equally effects
this suspension in a mode that annuls or tempers its own effect" (1982, p. 8). The
idea of the detour as a suspension describes shifts in the patient's clinical narrative

as a process of binding libidinal impulses and investing in shared, symbolic activity. By associating to the material he has produced, the patient suspends the immediacy of wish-fulfillment in enactment in the interest of associative linking and the possibility of interpretation. This is the link between the Freudian notion of binding (*Bindung*) and the Derridean notion of writing as the inscription of the differance between the material and the ideal. In *The Post Card: From Socrates to Freud and Beyond* (1987), Derrida demonstrates that Freud's description of the relation to reality in *Beyond the Pleasure Principle* (1920), where the principle of reality is understood as a modification of the pleasure principle— as "the temporary toleration of unpleasure as a step on the long indirect road to pleasure"—and not in terms of some given opposition between pleasure and reality, indicates that Freudian psychoanalysis functions inadvertently as a deconstruction of metaphysical, subject/object structures. In response to Freud's understanding of reality here Derrida writes, "Here we are touching upon the point of greatest obscurity, on the very enigma of differance, on precisely that which divides its very concept by means of a strange cleavage. We must not hasten to decide" (1982, p. 19). To decide in favor of the reality principle—or, alternatively, the pleasure principle—would be to forgo the ability to tolerate the tension of theoretical or therapeutic *play* as the differance between the two.

This last point warrants a return to Winnicott's work and to the specific questions it stakes out around the concepts of play, culture, space and transition. As discussed above, playing, in Winnicott's sense, occurs/resides neither inside nor outside the realm of the child's experience, rather it resists the opposition between the two in such a way that forces us to rethink the relationship between inside and outside, subject and object. The effects of this force on Winnicott's texts produce a startling series of insights and challenges to the conventional, commonsense way of conceiving of the mother–infant relationship. To wit, the mother's role in providing "protective postponement and dosed stimulation" (Ogden 1986, p. 170), measured in terms of time and thereby creating mental space, allows for the gradual disillusionment of weaning. The internalization of the mother's soothing function establishes the mother as neither present nor absent for the infant, or rather as both present and absent "at the same time." In other words, the mother's status in the child's universe exceeds the opposition of presence and absence which regulates all our thinking about the objective realities of time and space. This exceeding of the opposition presence/absence in both its spatial and temporal configurations allows for the development of the capacity to be alone, and as Ogden puts it, "In the development of the capacity to be alone, the infant develops the ability *to generate the space in which he lives*" (1986, p. 182; emphasis added). The generation of subjective space as the temporalization of existence is facilitated by the mother's introduction of various means by which to organize difference.

In this sense, we can say that Winnicott's developmental schema, particularly as it is developed by Ogden, is a schema of *differantial* development. The concepts of "holding the infant over time" and of "continuity (in time) of environment" intimate the complex interactions of spatial and temporal metaphors in any attempt

**30** Difference and psychic space

to represent the infant's experience. The concept of psychic space resists this complexity if it is understood non-dynamically and without complementary reference to a conceptualization of something like psychic time, which would not be simply a seriality of states of self-awareness, as some authors (e.g. Mitchell 1993; Bromberg 1998) have been influential in having proposed. In the same way that we are driven to impose the inadequate terms mother and infant on the mother–infant matrix in order to think its developmental dynamics, so we are driven to impose the model of physical space on our understanding of the psyche, where a more rigorous interpretation would need to think the relationship between psychic space and time, as between mother and infant, as differance.

It is also possible to elaborate a theory of the therapeutic relationship along similar lines. Once again, Winnicott's work, via certain themes which anticipate and are developed independently by Derrida, opens up a possible pathway. According to Winnicott in a famous passage:

> Psychotherapy takes place in the overlap of two areas of playing, that of the patient and that of the therapist. Psychotherapy has to do with two people playing together. The corollary of this is that where playing is not possible then the work done by the therapist is directed towards bringing the patient from a state of not being able to play into a state of being able to play.
>
> (1971, p. 39)

It is important to recognize here that this is no mere metaphor. Winnicott is not simply comparing the therapeutic process with children's play. Playing, again, for Winnicott has a very specific sense, one which is altogether different from that understood by a behavioral approach to play as an activity specific to childhood. He insists on a "significant distinction between the meanings of the noun 'play' and the verbal noun 'playing'" (1971, p. 40), emphasizing that playing must be thought without determinate reference to its contents. Child observation is inclined to attend to the themes with which children's play concerns itself rather than the sense of playing as a "thing in itself." Thus, for Winnicott, "There is something about playing that has not yet found a place in the psychoanalytic literature" (p. 41).

What does it mean to bring the patient into a state of being able to play, and how might one understand such a clinical achievement? Winnicott describes an inability to play elsewhere by distinguishing between elaborative dreaming on the one hand and repetitive fantasying on the other: "Dream fits into object-relating in the real world, and living in the real world fits into the dream-world in ways familiar to psychoanalysts. By contrast, however, fantasying remains an isolated phenomenon, absorbing energy but not contributing-in either to dreaming or to living" (1971, p. 26). In response to a patient who fantasized about people entering and taking over her apartment, and who subsequently dreamt that this was happening, he explains:

> The *fantasy* had to do with some people coming in and taking over her flat. That is all. The *dream* that people came and took over her flat would have to

do with her finding new possibilities in her own personality... [F]antasying was about a certain subject and it was a dead end. *It had no poetic value.* The corresponding dream, however, *had poetry in it,* that is to say, layer upon layer of meaning related to past, present, and future, and to inner and outer, and always fundamentally about herself. It is this poetry of the dream that is missing in her fantasying and in this way it is impossible for me to give meaningful interpretations about fantasying.

(1971, p. 35; emphases in original)

Winnicott further maintains that, "It will be observed that a time factor is operative which is different according to whether [the patient] is fantasying or imagining. In the fantasying, what happens happens immediately, except that it does not happen at all" (p. 27). His patient is "stuck" in a mode of organizing experience in such a way that by persistently "fantasying" that things are happening, nothing actually happens—life experiences pass by in a seemingly unconnected sequence of "nows" lacking the richness of a historical narrative relating past, present and future in any consequential way. Gradual success in the treatment later allowed the patient to make "some excursions into imaginative planning of the future which seemed to give a prospect of future happiness that was different from the here-and-now fixity of any satisfaction that there can be in fantasying" (p. 35). This "here-and-now fixity" concerns the immediacy of presence as an isolated and narrow mode of relating to oneself and to the world. Fantasying, rather than allowing for an enrichment of reality in the way that dreaming or playing does by motivating action, substitutes for reality and paralyzes action. This is why Winnicott judges it impossible to interpret where this fixity persists. Playing involves tolerating the possibility that immediate experience might be open to different interpretations, such that different experiences might follow. Where playing is not possible, experience is only as it appears at present, without being open to a future over the course of which change might occur. What is lacking where playing has been foreclosed upon is a capacity for symbolization as the ability to transmute immediate, sensory events into meaningful experiences embedded in one's sense of personal history and collective tradition—that is, the ability to generate the space in which we live.

If bringing a patient to a state of being able to play involves unhinging his fixation on the here-and-now immediacy of objectively present experience such that other interpretations of experience become possible, what Winnicott is advocating here is quite similar to what Derrida had elaborated as the deconstruction of the uncritical privilege of self- presence characteristic of Western metaphysics. Winnicott sees a fixation on the here-and-now as determining an inability to symbolize one's experience and to engage in a therapeutic process. Similarly, what Derrida demonstrates in his readings of the texts that comprise the Western canon is a persistent, uncritical privilege of the voice and of consciousness according to which discursive propositions and possibilities are determined as self-evident truths.

## 32 Difference and psychic space

If thinking differance—that is, thinking non-oppositionally, which is what it means to think deconstructively—upsets this privilege of the present and of consciousness, it might then be an effective way of thinking clinically about unconscious processes. As "the 'thought-that-means-nothing,' the thought that exceeds meaning and meaning-as-hearing-oneself speak by interrogating them," differance is "the thought for which there is no sure opposition between outside and inside" (Derrida 1981, p. 12). Derrida's quasi-substantive differance in this sense attempts to thematize something comparable to Winnicott's "verbal noun" playing: "To risk meaning nothing is to start to play, and first to enter into the play of differance" (p. 14). To risk meaning nothing is first to risk the possibility that what one intends to say or to mean is not in effect what one means, that what is meant in what is said is other than what is consciously intended or calculated. Differance would thus describe what originally orders the apparently pure spontaneity of meaning so that meaning may be both identical to itself and always other than itself, so that what is said is able to convey meaning yet always be open to the possibility that what has been said might mean something else entirely. This is the structural possibility of symbolizing one's individual experience, as well as the possibility that encouraging symbolization might constitute the basis for a therapeutic technique.

## Psychology as ontology

As the following chapters will elaborate and attempt to make increasingly clear, conceiving of the analytic relationship in terms of differance, playing or spacing requires that we expand our thinking about the mutative function of interpretation in helping the patient to organize the differences between his or her psychic structure and that of the analyst. As itself an organization of differences, psychic structure too would have to be understood as a kind of play, as Winnicott proposes in stating that treatment "takes place in the overlap of two areas of playing," and as Derrida suggested on several occasions (1978, 1982). Such an approach to treatment as an ongoing, playful suspension of reality into the productions of fantasy for the purpose of expansive exploration—exploring the differences between reality and fantasy as the "space" or matrix of a symbolizing attitude—would demand new approaches to the meanings of the concepts of the unconscious and of defense, particularly as they have been historically determined and limited by spatial frameworks of representation. What could thereby be opened up to is a thinking, and perhaps a practice, that follows not on our envisioning a dialectic between consciousness and the unconscious that engenders symbols, but on an understanding of how promoting the play of symbolization produces effects of consciousness and unconsciousness coordinated differantially.

In one of his best moments of provocative insight, Winnicott (1971) writes, "In psychology, the idea of interchange is based on an illusion in the psychologist" (p. 12). A problem is lodged at the center of our relation to the very object of psychoanalytic investigation: the idea of interchange, of what is today loudly trumpeted as intersubjectivity, the relationship between separate minds. The word "illusion" here must be figured in its specifically Winnicottian sense. By marking out an area of illusion, Winnicott is not criticizing a potentially remediable error, rather he is indicating that there is a transitional area within our own theorizing. In any attempt to describe the interchange between mother and infant, this transitional area asserts itself. Developmental theory therefore requires more than a merely intersubjective account of the mother and infant relationship; it requires a complex symbolic account of that relationship determined by a rigorous theoretical exploration of this transitional area inherent to any conceptual approach. That is, certain unconscious elements are at work in our theorizing which consistently return us to a metaphysical thinking in terms of subjects and objects, which undermines any effort to provide a comprehensive representation of the infant's experience, and which must be accounted for.

While Winnicott's statement is directed at the psychologist as observer of the mother-infant relationship, it is also implicitly addressed to the psychologist as clinician intervening in the patient's discourse, whatever limits the comparison of the therapist-patient and mother-infant relationships involves. If the idea of interchange involves illusion on the part of the one who attempts to theorize interchange as such, then this illusion is installed at the core of the therapeutic relationship, where the clinician's efforts at intervention are guided by his or her own symbolization of the differences between himself or herself and the patient. Every instance of clinical intervention—interpretive, empathic, instructional, pharmacological, etc.—reflects the therapist's capacity to organize these differences between himself or herself and the patient who receives its effects. Metapsychology, as an attempt to conceptualize the relationship between these differences, organizes and directs the form of interpretive therapeutic intervention. Against those who would encourage us to abandon theory in favor of a more "experience near" approach then, it must be asserted that metapsychology, no less than the analysis of the transference and counter-transference, is an attempt at symbolizing the therapeutic relationship.

Intrinsic to the structure of classical metapsychology is the idea of the solipsistically individuated mind, on which the concept of intersubjectivity or interchange is predicated. As Derrida consistently argued, and as the written work of many authors from various psychoanalytic perspectives across the professional field bears witness to, the form of this predication is not simple. The illusion of interchange continuously inserts an image of relatedness prior to any instance of individuation. This operation is perhaps already expressed in the conceptualization of mind as self-reflective: as fundamentally related to itself, interchanging with itself, and thus as dynamically other than itself—becoming itself in becoming-other-than itself. This self-effacing dynamic would also provide opportunities for illusion, transition and play.

If theory itself harbors certain transitional areas, these areas can be more or less complex, more or less differentiated—their "space" can be more or less open. In conceiving of psychic or inner space, we are constantly at risk of proposing a kind of interior bubble in which the subject and his or her world reside. We lose too much of the richness of experience this way by taking the metaphor of

**34** Difference and psychic space

psychic space literally, where this space is thought of as a canvas or background state against which internal dynamics get played out or within which internal objects are installed. Instead, psychic space might better be approached as a dynamism in its own right, one which shapes both the individual mind and the external world with which it interacts, as well as any discursive attempt to depict their relationship. To represent this movement otherwise, in Derridean terms as "the becoming-time of space or the becoming-space of time," is to begin to consider the therapeutic action of psychoanalysis as an intervention not merely at the psychological but at the ontological level.

## References

Bromberg, P. (1998). *Standing in the Spaces*. Hillsdale, NJ: The Analytic Press.

Derrida, J. (1973). *Speech and Phenomena*. Trans. D. Allison. Evanston, IL: Northwestern University Press.

Derrida, J. (1976). *Of Grammatology*. Trans. G. Spivak. Baltimore, MD: Johns Hopkins University Press.

Derrida, J. (1978). *Writing and Difference*. Trans. A. Bass. Chicago, IL: University of Chicago Press.

Derrida, J. (1981). *Positions*. Trans. A. Bass. Chicago, IL: University of Chicago Press.

Derrida, J. (1982). *Margins—of Philosophy*. Trans. A. Bass. Chicago, IL: University of Chicago Press.

Derrida, J. (1987). *The Post Card—From Socrates to Freud and Beyond*. Trans. A. Bass. Chicago, IL: University of Chicago Press.

Ferenczi, S. (1913). "Stages in the Development of the Sense of Reality." *First Contributions to Psychoanalysis*. New York: Bruner-Mazel, 1980.

Freud, S. (1915). "The Unconscious." S.E. 14.

Freud, S. (1920). *Beyond the Pleasure Principle*. S.E. 18.

Heidegger, M. (1969). *Identity and Difference*. Trans. J. Stambaugh. Chicago, IL: University of Chicago Press.

Heidegger, M. (1972). *On Time and Being*. Trans. J. Stambaugh. Chicago, IL: University of Chicago Press.

Loewald, H. (1962). "Superego and Time." *Papers on Psychoanalysis*. New Haven, CT: Yale University Press, 1980.

Loewald, H. (1972). "The Experience of Time." *Papers on Psychoanalysis*. New Haven, CT: Yale University Press, 1980.

Mitchell, S. (1993). *Hope and Dread in Psychoanalysis*. New York: Basic Books.

Ogden, T. (1986). *The Matrix of the Mind*. Northvale, NJ: Jason Aronson.

Plotnitsky, A. (1994). *Complementarity*. Durham, NC: Duke University Press.

Saussure, F. (1959). *Course in General Linguistics*. Trans. W. Baskin. New York: McGraw-Hill.

Segal, H. (1957). "Notes on Symbol Formation." *International Journal of Psychoanalysis* 38: 391–397.

Winnicott, D.W. (1960). "The Theory of the Parent-Infant Relationship." *The Maturational Processes and the Facilitating Environment*. New York: International Universities Press, 1965.

Winnicott, D.W. (1971). *Playing and Reality*. New York: Routledge.

# 2

# THE SPECTRALITY OF THE CLINICAL FRAME

In the previous chapter I introduced Derrida's notoriously obscure term *differance* in order to demonstrate that—its neologistic aspects and the difficulties facing its translation for a non-French speaking audience notwithstanding—what it attempts to describe is an experience of development, relationality and transformation that is not unfamiliar to psychoanalysts but for which we do not possess our own rigorous vocabulary. Lacking such a conceptual vocabulary, psychoanalysis is all the more disempowered when called to account for itself. Unlike forms of treatment that are widely supported by mental health organizations and academic research funds, psychoanalysis does not provide topical solutions to problems posed by entrenched forms of cognitive or behavioral pathology. Psychoanalysis is not a managerial strategy, it does not help the subject better to manage his or her symptomatic or destructive thinking or behavior. Rather, an analysis aims at the fundamental transformation of the subject himself or herself, and in such a way that less symptomatic and more creative and rewarding forms of thinking and behaving will inevitably follow.

In this way, the psychoanalytic clinic provokes and cultivates processes of differentiation and individuation; it does not merely provide self-knowledge and understanding. This is what I meant at the end of the last chapter, and in anticipation of a more in-depth discussion of Heidegger's role in deconstructive thinking in this and later chapters, when I said that the kind of deeply individuating, differentiating transformations that occur over the course of an analytic process take place at the level not of psychology but of ontology—in the way the patient *is,* even in the absence of conscious reflection or self-understanding. The aim of this chapter is to demonstrate how an examination of the concept of the clinical frame provides a lever for opening up this way of thinking about the therapeutic action of psychoanalysis.

**36** The spectrality of the clinical frame

## Symbolization as differance and the frame as writing

Recall Derrida's statement from his 1968 essay "Differance," cited in the previous chapter:

> An interval must separate the present from what it is not in order for the present to be itself, but this interval that constitutes it as present must, by the same token, divide the present in and of itself, thereby also dividing, along with the present, everything that is thought on the basis of the present, that is, in our metaphysical language, every being, and singularly substance or the subject. In constituting itself, in dividing itself dynamically, this interval is what might be called *spacing*, the becoming-time of space or the becoming-space of time (temporization).
>
> (1982, p. 13)

Differance as *spacing*—the becoming-time of space, the becoming-space of time—is intrinsic to the differentiating function that makes symbolization possible. This cannot be the basis of an exclusively cognitive faculty. In order to be experienced symbolically, something must be both itself and other than itself—it must be itself in differing from itself, opening itself up by deferring any ultimate closure of its identity—and we must experience ourselves both as ourselves and as different from ourselves in order to think symbolically. Symbolization as a capacity cultivated in the human mind is an open encounter with the differentiating function at the heart of the symbolic thing. Conceived in this way, symbolization is not something the mind does to an inert, meaningless, material object—it *is* the encounter between mind and thing, both of which would have to contain within themselves auto-differentiating, self-symbolizing processes.[1]

One way of stating this would be to say that symbolization is possible because both the symbolizing mind and the symbolized thing exist in space and time. To be effectively rigorous we would have to say that by existing "in" time and space what we really mean is that mind and thing *are* spatializing and temporalizing, and that this is what it means to say that they are individuating: both mind and thing are processes tending towards individuation and singularity, and *always in relation to one another*. To speak literally as if minds and things exist objectively "inside" time and space—like water in a glass, in Heidegger's example (1996, p. 50; see below)—would imply that both minds and things could exist in isolation "outside" time and space, and thus outside the impossibly complex fabric of their relations with one another. Minds and things would have no meaningful existence outside this fabric, without each bearing the trace of the other as the form of its relationship to itself. Instead we must think their existence as irreducibly spatial(izing) and temporal(izing). This would be to think difference and relation as possessed of the same categorical, ontological status that we attribute to time and space in an everyday sense. To say that mind and world exist "in" time and space is a way of symbolizing our experience, one that is very easy to take for granted and to think in a concrete, desymbolized way.

To conceive of minds and things as spatializing and temporalizing is not so difficult a thought as Derrida's reputation would lead us to believe. His privileged example was always *writing* understood as a technical practice of repetition, translation and differentiation. Reading and writing are processes that occur at the boundary between the subjective and the objective, or between the psychical and the material. What Derrida had intended to illuminate was how these common, everyday practices (which are nonetheless extremely fragile and capable of being made inaccessible to us) demonstrate that any such boundary is dynamic and constantly in flux—that it is never absolute and cannot ultimately authorize a logic of opposition when thinking about the relationship between mind and world.

When I write something down, my consciousness, which does not exist in the world as a spatial object but as an immaterial, temporal flow, is translated into something that is static and that exists spatially as "out there" in the world, as something that is written down. Writing converts the time of consciousness into the space of the written word. This is an example of what Derrida means by "the becoming-space of time." Through the practice of writing, my thoughts or the temporal process of my thinking is inscribed materially as spatial characters elaborated across a page, and this occurs according to a particular tradition to which I belong or which I have made my own in having learned how to read and to write. Retrieving the living experience of consciousness from the dead letter of the written word involves retemporalizing what has become spatial in the act of writing. This is what the act of reading consists in: "the becoming-time of space." Writing spatializes something temporal, reading temporalizes something spatial. When we are writing we are always simultaneously reading, repeating these gestures of translation in a way that cultivates our individuality—which is to say our *literacy*, without which individuation is not possible. Reading and writing are particularly powerful forms of this process which is yet in no way limited to them. By means of the ongoing repetition of the gestures of reading and writing—as gestures and concepts which therefore must be thought in an expanded sense— emerges the possibility of literacy, according to which reading and writing, like time and space themselves, are understood or held together not as opposed but as intimately connected to one another, and in such a way that to speak of them as separate-but-connected demands a new, non-classical thinking about relationality as individuation and as differance.

The analytic frame implicitly involves a consideration of the meaning of the experience of space and time, even if this is not made explicit by clinicians themselves, either in practice or in theory. In all other forms of psychological treatment, the patient goes to the office where the therapist practices his or her particular technique, and the setting itself is irrelevant to that practice. The non-analytic therapist is a specialist in possession of a certain body of knowledge from which issues a certain skill set, and the office is simply the place where he or she exercises those technical skills. The setting is so unimportant as a background to the point that, in some therapeutic modalities, it can be transposed to a radio broadcast, podcast or television studio. This would be unthinkable for the psychoanalytic clinician, and

**38** The spectrality of the clinical frame

this reflects a different though again largely unarticulated meaning of the concept of "technique" specific to psychoanalysis.[2]

In an analysis, the office itself is a part of the therapeutic technique, as is the activity of attending the sessions, and as is the analyst himself or herself in practicing the stance of interpretive neutrality. Analytic technique is not merely something the analyst does, as some activity among other everyday activities; it is something the analyst and the environment he or she creates merges into and embodies. Should the analytic frame be considered itself a part of analytic technique? And if this were to be the case, what exactly do we mean by "technique" in psychoanalysis, in contrast to other forms of psychological treatment?

Of course, the clinical frame cannot legitimately be considered itself a practice, or rather it is not exclusively a set of practices, as it includes, in addition to the practices gathered under the term neutrality, the spatial arrangement of objects in the room: the analyst's chair and the direction in which it is oriented; the couch that belongs to the patient and to the analyst, in different but essential ways; the tissue box, the clock, the pillow—all of which are potentially subject to transferential investments. In addition, the temporal arrangement of the fixed scheduling of analytic appointments is also a crucial part of the frame. The frame is thus certainly not a merely theoretical concept, yet it requires a very rigorous effort at theorizing in order to make a properly psychoanalytic clinical practice possible. This would not be a theory upon which the analyst might pontificate, but a theory that he or she must—according to a word that always circulates in discussions of the frame and whose meaning will have to be clarified—*hold*. The frame inhabits the border between psychoanalytic practice and psychoanalytic theory, concretizing but also articulating their differences—differences between the practical and the theoretical, the material and the ideal, which are revealed to be other than simply opposed to one another by means of a clinical practice like interpretation. This is also where psychoanalysis distinguishes itself from academic theory and establishes itself as a transformative, therapeutic discipline.

The nature of the clinical frame turns out to be rather difficult to define because it challenges basic, commonsense assumptions, both psychoanalytic and otherwise. When analysts talk about the frame they are generally referring to a set of coordinates and practices that allow the analyst and patient together to distinguish between what the analysis *is* and what it *is not*— between the *time* when the analysis is occurring and when it is not, and between the *space* where it occurs and where it does not. Not infrequently patients begin sessions with statements such as, "Since I last saw you what's happened is…" or, "I was thinking about last time and…" What is implicitly being communicated is that now we are back in the space and time of analysis, now it is happening *again*—something is being repeated, and what is being repeated emerges from out of and makes itself clear by means of the act of repetition. The continuity that has been broken in the interruption between sessions now has been reestablished, things can go on as if there had been no break, nothing dividing us from one another in the time that we have chosen to take up together with one another. This occurs even if the break between sessions has been particularly disruptive and has been experienced as a rupture or loss. The frame thus conjoins the analytic process with the patient's outside life while strictly differentiating them, and it does so through practices of repetition: coming to the same place, at the same times, over and over again. This is the ceremonial aspect of the frame that integrates conjunction and disjunction, continuity and difference, in order to facilitate the sense that there is an ongoing process taking place. Having to leave and to return to the office can feel like disruptions of this process, when in fact they are constitutive of it.

Holding the frame can be considered a mode of psychoanalytic technique, but how are we to think about the status of the frame itself? As what marks the difference between analytic experience and non-analytic experience, or between the treatment and "real life" (according to an opposition that it both respects and at the same time moves into crisis), the analytic frame functions as a form of technological support that allows for the emergence and development of an analytic process. It is not typical to consider the frame as a form of technology—the very idea of a "psychoanalytic technology" is likely to appear even inherently strange. For the moment, what I mean is simply that, just as an automobile functions as a form of technological support that allows us to journey from one destination to another, so the clinical frame makes the analytic process *possible* without itself being an *actual* part of that process. This is also perhaps why, like the car that supports our traveling and about which we do not think much unless it breaks down (and if we do consciously think about it too much while we are driving, we are likely to cause such breakdown in the form of an accident), the analytic literature tends to the question of the clinical frame almost exclusively where breakdowns in the functioning of the frame occur. The Argentinian analyst José Bleger addressed this in a seminal paper to which I will turn in the most substantial section of this chapter.

The basic function of the analytic frame is the coordination of space and time: again, the patient is invited to come to the same place (the analyst's office), at the same times (according to a set schedule), over and over again for an unspecified (open) amount of time. Of course there are always discontinuities in this structure (cancellations, vacations, the analyst may move from one office to another, etc.), but it is the commitment to maintaining regularity through spatial and temporal repetition that opens up the possibility of an analytic process. The fact that the patient has to travel to and from the office, perhaps over considerable distances sometimes, is in ambiguous and peripheral ways itself a part of the frame, as is the fact that the time of the meetings are set and while flexibility is not ruled out it is crucial that the time remain fixed even if this causes disruption of other activities which either the patient or the analyst might momentarily find more enjoyable.

What I have called the ceremonial aspect of the frame, as this is composed of fundamental acts of practical repetition that create the possibility of therapeutic difference, also involves a certain disciplinary regimen. Holding the frame means imposing a high degree of stability with respect to the timing and regularity of the analytic appointments, as well as restricting interactions between patient and

**40** The spectrality of the clinical frame

analyst outside the consulting room. This can feel like a very authoritarian stance from the perspective of the patient in transference, as well as for the candidate learning to conduct analyses for the first time. As an aspect of analytic neutrality, the practice of holding the frame has become associated with a rigid, "classical Freudian" approach, and this has been the subject of endless attacks, particularly by those who adhere to interpersonal and relational perspectives today. I imagine this is because there has been a great deal of "classical" insistence on maintaining the frame in the absence of any thoughtful attempt to account for why or how this effort can itself function in an intrinsically therapeutic way, beyond protecting both patient and analyst from transferential and counter-transferential enactments and boundary violations. Because a classical, neutral frame has historically, inadequately been thought to be extrinsic to the work of interpretation—as supporting the work of interpretation but not as intrinsically interpretive in itself—the classical frame has not been considered itself a part of the mutative relationship, and a theory of the analytic relationship as mutative but non-interpretive (i.e. empathic) has become popular. As a result there has been a considerable amount of discussion about the therapeutic value of dispensing with the properly analytic frame (through self-disclosure, for example), but none grounded in a thinking about the frame as the way in which psychoanalysis provides a unique and unusual discipline for organizing time and space so as to make possible therapeutic transformation by means of the opening up of hitherto foreclosed symbolic processes. That is, crucial to the neutral frame as what allows the patient to symbolize previously unsymbolized experience is the practice of coming to the same place, at the same time, over and over again, for a period the length of which cannot be anticipated or controlled in advance. This is not just about stability, it is about opening up différance as the dynamic essence of individuating, symbolic processes through practices of spatial and temporal repetition.

In the previous chapter I demonstrated how deconstruction conceives of mind precisely as this opening, and not in terms of the familiar figure of the self-enclosed, psychological, Cartesian subject, whether intersubjectively oriented or not. This non-metaphysical, non-dialectical, processive way of thinking self-experience can be put together with a consideration of the clinical frame as an effort at temporalizing space and spatializing time, such that the efforts of psychoanalysis to open up the symptomatically foreclosed transitional time-space of symbolization can be regarded as an encounter with the differantial constitution of phenomenal experience itself. A psychoanalytic understanding of the self or subject informed by deconstruction situates symbolizing processes not as mere cognitive functions but as ontological structures constitutive of the experiences of self and world. That is, symbolization is to be understood not as something we *do* but as something we *are.* Grasping this involves an understanding of the intrinsically interpretive nature of the neutral clinical frame, revealing a coincidence of mind and environment beyond the reductions and mystifications of a classical metaphysics of presence.[3] As a result, the therapeutic action of psychoanalysis can be brought newly into focus and reevaluated.

## Heidegger and the frame: existential space-time

Before turning to the analytic literature on the nature of the clinical frame, and in order to weave together the discourses of psychoanalysis and deconstruction for the purpose of further demonstrating their inherent proximity, a brief overview of certain aspects of Heidegger's work—as the most important forerunner of Derrida's own, and as that of one of the key figures in the formulation of the project of deconstruction, alongside Nietzsche and Freud—is necessary. In Heidegger's "existential" thinking about space and time it is possible to discover new ways of thinking about the function of the "classical" stance of analytic neutrality.

In *Being and Time* (1996), Heidegger offers a framework for thinking about experience that is not grounded in claims about subjectivity and objectivity or any absolute opposition between them. In order to reconceive the nature of subjectivity as the existential structure Da-sein (literally, "being-there"—there is no way to translate this ordinary German word), he proceeds by cataloguing the ways in which human beings exist "in" the world or "in" time. From the outset Heidegger problematizes what exactly is meant by this sense of "in." The German *Da-sein* indicates not just being-there in the sense of being objectively present in time and space, but being-there in the way that a friend promises always to be there for us, indicating care (*Sorge*) and not possession, and in a way that is simultaneously both active and passive. Da-sein relates to its environment intimately in the way that a friend is *there*, ready to act yet without a predetermined agenda, actively waiting in response to need without imposing a preconceived solution. With this, *Being and Time* attempts to think beyond the oppositional logic of subjects and objects that drives modern technological science.

Heidegger's most general claim is that our experience demonstrates that time cannot be thought of as a series of successive punctual "nows." Time is not only the medium of development and change, our experience of time itself changes and develops. Time can appear to pass very slowly or very quickly depending on how we comport ourselves and what we are up to. Time understood as a progressive series of identical "nows" began as an abstract philosophical interpretation of time and has since become common sense, so much so that to challenge it would seem unusual and obscure. To the contrary, Heidegger demonstrates that this interpretation is itself confused, that time cannot be understood as three separate dimensions essentially distinct from one another, each bearing the form of objective presence: the now, the past as a now that is no longer now, and the future as a now that is yet to come but which can be calculated in advance as eventually a now. This "vulgar" understanding of time as a forward march through successive, isolated moments conceals a dynamic sense of time in which the present cannot be assigned priority, and in which past, present, and future are dynamically integrated. Heidegger's name for this is "ecstatic temporality." Time is ecstatic in the sense that it stands perpetually outside itself, always projecting itself forward towards the future that it *is* in an existential sense. This is the historical time of meaningfully lived human experience.

**42** The spectrality of the clinical frame

Unlike subjects and objects, Da-sein does not exist in a punctual form modeled on the here-and-now of objective presence, but as a stretching-along that reaches beyond itself towards its future, individuating or "temporalizing" itself by means of its projects and desires. Human beings are unique in that they are beings capable of becoming concerned with their future—being-there in such a way that this is experienced as meaningful. Heidegger describes interest in and concern for the future as Da-sein's "being-ahead-of-itself-in-already-being-in-a-world" and as "always-being-together-with others" (p. 179). What this means is that human beings are not *first* subjects who are *then* subsequently set loose within an objective world alongside others. Rather, our ways of being—of existing and acting in an everyday sense that is so easy to take for granted—are determined by an essential openness to our environment. This openness is the condition of possibility of both meaning and desire, and for Heidegger it is also a source of anxiety and of the sense of uncanniness. Being-in-a-world-with others is not a subjective quality I possess but an existential structure I am: Da-sein does not "have" relationships with others, it *is* that dynamic relationality that Heidegger calls ecstatic. This has nothing to do with notions of intersubjectivity, which consistently fail to think the relational by subordinating it to the interpersonal. We are not, in Heidegger's example, in-the-world like water is in a glass (p. 50); the *thereness* of human existence is intrinsically temporal, open, incalculable, free. This is not a freedom "I have," but a freedom one *is* prior to any determination of subjective identity. According to Heidegger, grasping this constitutes "the most radical *individuation*" (p. 34; emphasis in original).

As abstruse as Heidegger's thinking might appear at first, what it can help clinicians to clarify—what can seem so obvious, but is so easily and often forgotten—is that a patient is not "in" analysis in the way that water is in a glass, but temporally *as* a process of ongoing evolution, development, and change. Where being in analysis is thought in a concrete or desymbolized way, this legitimizes hierarchical models of treatment in which the analyst holds himself up as the superior ego with whom the patient should identify, because it implies that while the patient is "in" analysis, the analyst occupies a position of authority and objective knowledge outside or above this process. That the analyst too is changed by the very nature of clinical work is disavowed. This occurs whenever the radically singular, individuating temporality of clinical processes is repudiated by a thinking that prioritizes the immediacy of objective presence. Such thinking is celebrated everywhere in contemporary culture, so much so that it has become absolutely blind to its own pathology. Psychoanalysis must not itself succumb to this blindness.

Thinking space and time concretely has the effect of accelerating our experience of time and of dedifferentiating our experience of space, preventing the world from functioning as a source of meaning and tradition. Heidegger describes this as a process according to which, "Everything gets lumped together into uniform distancelessness" (1971b, p. 164). For Heidegger, thinking in this way is not a merely theoretical failure, it is an existential crisis that threatens us globally given the increasingly quantitative, calculative rendering of all political, economic and cultural experience today:

All distances in times and space are shrinking. Man now reaches over-night, by plane, places which formerly took weeks and months of travel. He now receives information, by radio, of events which he formerly learned about only years later, if at all. The germination and growth of plants, which remained hidden throughout the seasons, is now exhibited publicly in a minute, on film. Distant sites of the most ancient cultures are shown on film as if they stood this very moment amidst today's street traffic. Moreover, the film attests to what it shows by presenting also the camera and its operators at work. The peak of this abolition of every possible remoteness is reached by television, which will soon pervade and dominate the whole machinery of communication.

(1971b, p. 163)

Pressure to accelerate time in order to calculate and to control the outcomes of one's commitments belongs to and drives the demand for incessant productivity specific to a culture of industrialized consumption. The time of consumption is time figured reductively as focused on the immediacy of the here-and-now. Like the addict whose past is lost and whose future feels hopelessly irrelevant, the con-sumer consciously or unconsciously calculates all efforts and engagements in goal-oriented terms toward the acts of acquiring, using, and devouring. This is a perverse form of internalization in which consumption–time is addiction–time. The question as to what one can expect to receive in return for one's investments valorizes now-time over and against any orientation to future possibility: I consume according to a demand that I can grasp in advance what it is that I am going to acquire and to experience in the act of consumption. Knowing in advance what it is I am going to get, and getting it in accordance with my predetermined knowledge, constitutes a circuit of satisfaction that provides me with a sense of having control over myself, my environment, and my future. This is an illusory sense of autonomy that both discourages the desire for change, and that conceals my increasing dependence on repeating the same gestures over and over again. The more accurately I can anticipate the pleasures of consumption, and the more those pleasures mirror my anticipation uninterruptedly (that is, the longer I am able to stay afloat financially), the more enclosed I become in this circuit as a system of narcissistic support. As a result, my investment in the past and future degenerates, and I become increas-ingly oriented towards endless repetition of the same. Consumption in this way consumes not only objects but our experience of the dynamic, durational structure of time itself. It is both addictogenic and chronolytic.

Unlike standardized treatments, the lengths of which can be relatively pro-grammed in advance and that are for this reason favored by insurance companies, psychoanalysis in its open, unpredictable temporality resists the time of consumption. The time of psychoanalysis—with its repetitively timed and spaced appointments, engendering an ongoing sense of duration, tradition and stability in the absence of any predetermined knowledge as to when a termination date can be expected—is intrinsically opposed to the now-time of consumption-addiction. It is this aspect

**44** The spectrality of the clinical frame

of the frame as open, incalculable structure (we don't know what will happen, or when exactly) that allows interpretation to function as something other than a pre-programmed, standardized procedure. Consumed with and by his symptoms, the patient is invited to invest his time and energy differently, by coming often and by observing the fundamental rule, and by not attempting to "figure himself out." This difference is indicated by the nature of the analytic frame: insistently repetitive (day after day, year after year, at the same time and place), analysis imitates the frame-work of consumption-addiction in order to repeat difference rather than identity. Thought deconstructively, the practice of holding a neutral frame is an effort to open up time toward future possibility rather than remain stuck in the empty time-lessness of the symptom's ruthless "now."

## Marion Milner: the temporal-spatial "framed gap"

The concept of the clinical frame can be traced in the psychoanalytic literature to an essay from 1952 by the British Independent analyst Marion Milner entitled, "The framed gap" (Milner 1987a). The essay is not a polished academic piece but an account of two lectures the author had given previously, the original texts of which appear either to have been lost or never to have existed in any formal sense in the first place. At a mere three pages, "The framed gap" is more on the order of a memoir, a memory of an idea that had never been fully fleshed out conceptually, and which is never thoroughly defined in the context of the essay itself but which would be seized upon by later authors—more often than not in the absence of any reference to Milner, as if the concept were so intuitive as to have always existed—as having articulated something crucial to grasping the nature of clinical work.

Milner builds her concept of the frame based upon an analogy to painting where the frame that borders the paper or canvas sets the work off as distinct from yet connected to the context in which it appears. She describes "the frame as some-thing that marked off what's inside it from what's outside it," comparable to "other human activities where the frame is essential … for instance the acted play, cere-monies, rituals, processions, even poems framed in silence when spoken and the space of the paper when written" (1987a, pp. 80–81). What unifies these practices is the frame as something that exists "in time as well as in space"—a quality equally essential, she says, to the nature of the analytic session.

With the word "session" we emphasize the temporal aspect of the discrete psychoanalytic event: a session refers to that which is timed. As a concept, the frame appears more spatial in its implication, but a part of what it describes is also the ongoing continuity of discretely organized sessions over time. The frame is composed of time (the regular and frequent scheduling of the sessions), but in such a way that makes it feel stable, like an object that occupies space. And yet the frame is also spatial in its manifestation (the office, the couch, the arrangement of objects such as clocks and tissue boxes in the room, the positions of the patient and analyst themselves, etc.), the stability of which manifests its temporal nature as an ongoing process.

The spectrality of the clinical frame **45**

In a paper she presented the same year in honor of Melanie Klein's seventieth birthday, Milner briefly returned to the concept of the frame in discussing the centrality of illusion in psychoanalytic experience. She wrote:

> The frame marks off the different kind of reality that is within it from that which is outside it; but a *temporal spatial frame* also marks off the special kind of reality of a psychoanalytic session. And in psychoanalysis it is the existence of this frame that makes possible the full development of that creative illusion that analysts call the transference.
>
> (1987b, p. 87; emphasis added)

Thus the frame—what Milner is compelled to qualify as a "temporal spatial frame," and it is this qualifying remark that demands critical attention—does not merely demarcate one object from another; it "marks off" a "special kind of reality" from an otherwise ordinary experience of reality. This "special kind of reality" is not the transference or is *not yet* the transference but is what makes possible the cultivation of the creative illusion of the transference which is the condition of the possibility of therapeutic interpretation. Without the frame that *marks* the difference between two realities there would be no transference properly speaking, and there would no possibility of an interpretive treatment.

Milner thus indicates that she grasps quite clearly that the analogy to the frame in painting makes it appear as if she is describing some circumscribed object, when in fact she is describing something that is itself an ongoing process, yet one that manifests a certain object-like stability. A "framed gap" risks being understood as the presence of an absence, but a "temporal spatial frame"—which is to say, something that is composed of time and space, and that therefore occupies neither properly speaking, yet without being simply non-existent—functions as a mark, an inscription. The temporal spatial frame inscribes a certain difference "between two realities" (notice that Milner herself does not indicate two different experiences of reality—my sense is that this is not an oversight or lack of clarity). The clinical frame concerns time and space in that the frame marks off a different time and space that both makes the analytic process possible and is an ancillary part of that process itself. But the frame, as what marks the difference between two times and two spaces, is itself temporal and spatial, and where Milner writes of a "temporal spatial frame" she is describing the clinical frame as something that is not just both temporal and spatial but something in which time and space are not so formally distinguishable from one another—a kind of time-space in which the difference between time and space is not yet absolute. This is Milner's debt to Winnicott: The frame belongs to and organizes the area of transitional *phenomena*, yet without being a transitional *object*. Like Winnicott's *playing*, Milner's "framed gap" or "temporal spatial frame" is a "verbal noun."

What the frame organizes is thus not something extrinsic to what is meant by the frame itself. What brackets off the time and space of the clinic as distinct from everyday reality is a kind of difference intrinsic to both time and space themselves and that both allows for and calls into question their respective identities

**46** The spectrality of the clinical frame

and differences. The frame does not exist "in" time and space, rather it exists *as* a particular organization of time and space, which are thus revealed to be other than strictly uniform or objectively constant and self-identical. This is an organization composed of and by acts of repetition. In that it serves to mark off or to differentiate two realities from one another, its own status with respect to reality is ambiguous. Inside the frame lies the ceremonial time-space of the analytic experience; outside the frame lies ordinary, everyday life. This mark also differentiates between two different experiences of time: "outside" the time of analysis the patient is beset by all sorts of responsibilities and engagements imposed by environmental demand; "inside" the session the patient is afforded time to languish, to remember, to reflect, or not. To use a vocabulary introduced in the previous chapter: The psychoanalytic frame is itself a form of auto-affection that organizes or that inscribes time and space themselves as auto-affective processes. This is what Milner indicates when she writes, "…all these frames show that what is inside has to be *perceived, interpreted* in a way different from what is outside; they *mark off* an area within which what we perceive has to be taken as a symbol, as metaphor, not literally" (p. 81; emphases added). As a differential mark operating at the border between perception and understanding, the frame is itself a form of non-verbal interpretation that provokes the patient to interpret not some symbolic content but the difference between the symbolic and the non-symbolic. A temporal spatial frame is the mark of interpretation as differentiation or of symbolization as differ*a*nce.

In that it is both temporal and spatial, the frame is constitutively both interpretive and inscriptive—conjoining time and space in a way that is prior to and that makes possible the analysis of any particular psychological or relational content. In both marking and appearing as the mark of the difference between an inside and an outside, the frame appears as this difference itself—as repetition. What occurs inside the frame can therefore appear intensively symbolic (this is the centrality of illusion on which Milner insists), as distinct from the ordinary reality that occurs outside, in the patient's everyday life. But it is this very difference between the ordinary and the symbolic that the frame works to generate, that can appear as such because of the gesture that marks off the one from the other. This is the possibility of an interpretable transference as the integration of repetition and difference: within the clinical frame I repeat my past in ways that make it possible to do so differently by means of the encounter with the neutral analyst who not only practices but who embodies an interpretive stance. Repeating my past intensively, transferentially inside the frame allows me to repeat difference in my ordinary life outside the frame—to be therapeutically transformed. By demonstrating that what is inside of it must be interpreted differently from what is outside of it, the frame—again as that which is both common and fundamental to stage plays, ceremonies and rituals, as well as to painting, drawing and writing, and to psychoanalysis—both separates and connects what appears inside and outside the possibility of interpretation. Beyond its status as a concept, the experience of the frame does not just make interpretation possible, it is itself a form of interpretation.

This is perhaps why Milner does not go out of her way to distinguish between the frame as a particular kind of object and the frame as a circumscribed set of practices. This absence of any formal distinction which defines the very concept—as a concept that is not easily distinguishable from either the object or the practices that it describes—still marks the concept of the frame in the contemporary literature. For Milner, the concept of the frame names not only "a blank space, a framed gap" as in painting, drawing or writing when one begins with an empty canvas or sheet of paper, but equally "a sacrifice of deliberative action or working to a plan, instead allowing the hand or eye to play with the medium" (p. 80). The frame frames a certain absence of rules, a "gap" that is not necessarily an absence of content so much as an absence of constraint—a gap that is not nothing in that it is overflowing with potential and therefore ultimately uncontainable. The picture that hangs on the gallery wall was once a blank sheet, an absence standing out against a present background. The frame in this sense is what allows for a distinction to be made between absence and presence, and it does so by simultaneously appearing and withdrawing into the background. The "framed gap" is not an absence nor even an absence made present but a kind of interval or *spacing* between presence and absence, something that can be made manifest but that functions best as long as it remains imperceptible or silent. As any clinician well knows, the frame is strongest when its stability renders it undetectable. The more it is explicitly talked about, the more it ephemerally dissolves. This is in direct contrast to everything we are given to understand about the nature of the "talking cure."

Perhaps this is also why, in defining the concept of the frame, Milner seems more concerned with how it functions for the analyst than with how it functions for the patient. In contemporary discussions where the frame is at issue most commentators are concerned with how the patient experiences the analyst's efforts to establish and to maintain a clinical frame, and of special concern is what occurs when the frame is broken and how the patient can be expected to react. Milner is more interested in what kind of clinical attitude is authorized by the establishment and maintenance of an analytic frame that is regular, stable, and demanding. The frame as the absent-presence or temporal spatial *mark* of the difference between what is symbolically interpretable and what is not engenders in the analyst different yet complementary forms of attention or attentiveness to the patient's demands, needs and desires. Characteristically, Milner compares these to the subjective states of creative artists for whom there are "two kinds of attention, both necessary, a wide unfocused state, and a narrow focused penetrating kind, and that the wide kind brought remarkable changes in perception and enrichment of feeling" (p. 81). In writing about her previous presentations on this topic, she recalls having quoted Cezanne on "the capacity to achieve unmindfulness," thereby implicitly harkening back to Freud's (1912) "evenly suspended attention" and anticipating Bion's (1967) "without memory and desire."

## 48 The spectrality of the clinical frame

## Derrida: the frame as *parergon* or "the circle *en abyme*"

In *The Truth in Painting* (1987) Derrida, like Milner, offers a meditation on the ontological status of the frame as it relates to the work of art (strangely, he is also guided by a quote from Cezanne). Like Heidegger (1971a) before him, Derrida's concern is with the ambiguous boundary between the work of art in the sense of the art object, the finished artistic product, and the *work* of art in the sense of the activities or workings, more or less active or passive, that go into artistic production. At issue is the relationship between the work as an object that occupies space and the work as a process that occurs over time.

Derrida is concerned in particular with the detritus that the work of art generates and that is concealed by the final artistic product but without which a work proper would not be possible—the minor workings in which the difference between the final work of art and the ordinary, everyday work of what it means to be an artist is worked out and worked through, by means of which the difference between the work as an object occupying space and the work as a process occurring over time is marked or inscribed. He designates this minor yet essential working with the unusual word *parergon*, which is neither a neologism nor a theoretical abstraction. Derrida is attempting to retrieve a word that had previously existed only marginally, that had largely gone unspoken yet the traces of which were still there to be discovered in dictionaries. This is in order to bring attention to a marginal yet familiar, everyday experience.

*Parergon* describes a work or a mode of working (*ergon*) that is ancillary to a larger working, but that is essential to the effectiveness of that larger working despite its capacity ultimately to be forgotten and discarded. An example would be Cezanne's private sketches and studies for what would subsequently become more definitive and historical works. *Parergon* describes what functions at the margins or limits of a defined and substantial work, a kind of quasi-work that lets the real work (of the production of art, in this instance) work, and without which no work would get done because the difference between work and non-work would never get underway. Painters will know this work in the form of sketches, scribbles, abandoned canvases that lead up to—in such a way as to make possible, but at the same time in a way that must be superseded and concealed by—the work of art proper. Writers will know this work by the sketches (in an apparently different, though not unrelated sense of the word), pages, notebooks, or today the endless proliferation of incomplete and abandoned fragmentary digital files on their computers (in the mode of what used to be called "word processors"—a term that has fallen out of fashion but that is worth recalling here) that prepare for but that are ultimately irrelevant once an essay, journal article or book is made present as an object.

*Parergon* names those minor, private workings that allow major works to function publicly. It is what turns the *work* of art into *a* work of art. It was Heidegger who first gave thought to this in the essay, "The Origin of the Work of Art," which is considered by the academic publishing industry to date from 1950, but which in reality began as a working by the author sometime between 1935 and 1937. *Parergon* names the subterranean, necessarily concealed workings of the artist in any medium, whose work only appears publicly as a celebrated object (painting, book, recording, etc.) to the extent that the work that goes into its production remains concealed, the traces of which are let go of, and in such a way that in certain cases encourages the metaphysical valorization of the work of art as an instantiation of the sublime. Often this is coordinated with the idealization of the artist as genius, as if the work of art were merely a matter of divine inspiration.

*Parergon* as a name for the frame is thus that which is not part of the work (*ergon*) but which is not outside of the work (*hors-d'oeuvre*) either. It describes a boundary, a liminal state in which work is produced but discarded, erased—a kind of work that is neither *the* work nor non-work but that serves to mark out the work of art from everyday life as in contrast to artistic practice. Derrida's proximity to Winnicott here again could not be more apparent: as transitional (active-passive), the frame as *parergon* is neither the work of art itself nor its absence; it names both an essential part of the work of art *and* what can be easily discarded—what *must* be discarded in order for the true or final work to appear as such, but without which that appearance could never take place. *Parergon* is not the work proper but the "trait" by means of which can be read the artist's signature, as something identifiable but that must retreat into the background in order for the work of art to work, which is to say to be distinguishable from the artist himself, otherwise we are not in the presence of art but of narcissistic self-indulgence (it is no wonder that so much art today dedicates itself to staging the question of this very difference, which is the difference between the work of art and the commodity).

Derrida writes, "*Between* the outside and inside, between the external and the internal edge-line, the framer and the framed, the figure and the ground, form and content, signifier and signified, and *so on* for any two-faced opposition. The trait thus divides in this place where it takes place" (1987, p. 12; emphases in original). The frame exists "in" or *as* the time and space that marks the difference of the work from the world that provides both its context and its meaning while being excluded from participating in this excess of meaning that makes the work and, in turn, the world stand out in its meaningfulness, which is to say in its ecstatic, auto-affective differance. This is the frame of the work of art that makes of the work a work*ing* while concealing this ongoing, processive dimension from the work's public if not from the artist himself or herself.

What Derrida draws attention to here is the fact that much of what goes on in the process of the *work* of art cannot be subsumed by the concept of artistic *production*. The difference between those activities that comprise the production of the work of art and those activities and productions that would seem peripheral and unimportant, aborted attempts at production that appear unrelated to the production of the final work, is not as clear or as distinct as we are ordinarily given to assume. The more general implication here is that the illusion that there is an absolute difference between the work of art and life "itself" is necessary for the work of art to appear at all, but in a way that makes this illusion both an effect of the work of art and its antecedent condition. The work of art (in both senses, as object and as process) emerges from out of a space or interval in which ordinary life and work

**50** The spectrality of the clinical frame

differ from themselves, in order to return to themselves in the form of the aesthetic, that is, the emergence or manifestation of the beautiful. For Derrida this movement of return reflects not just artistic production but the nature of the psychical as such:

> No doubt art figures one of those productions of mind thanks to which the latter returns to itself, comes back to consciousness and cognizance and comes to its proper place by *returning* to it, in a circle. What is *called* [*s'appelle*: lit. "calls itself"] mind is that which says to itself "come" only to hear *itself* already saying "come back." The mind is what it is, says what it means, only *by returning*. Retracing its steps, in a circle.
>
> (1987, p. 26; emphases in original)

If we stay with him on his own terms for a moment, what Derrida is indicating is that the work of art is not one among many workings of the mind, rather it is one of those ways of working through which the mind discloses the way in which it itself operates. The artist loses himself in the work, sketching and drawing, for example, without any predetermined goal or intention. Much time is spent in the studio creating without knowing exactly *what* one intends to create, only *that* one intends to create, and as a result a good deal of paper, ink, paint, canvas, etc. is used up in work that will not appear "productive" according to a certain meaning typically assigned to this term.

Derrida's argument here is that the mind operates in much the same way: it loses itself, is taken up with seemingly nonsensical questions and concerns, goes outside of itself and forgets itself in order to wander the world aimlessly at times; it is not always productive according to a judgment from which it often suffers, especially today. But this lack of insistent productivity is in fact intrinsic to the structure of thought itself, and it is necessary for thinking in the form of an *open* mind that, in order to remain open, which is to say creative, must periodically lose itself in order to return to itself, in order to constitute a circle. This circle is not that of the self-enclosed Cartesian subject but a circle constituted by a passage through the world, through an ongoing and repetitive loss of self in thought. This circle is not solipsistic, it does not clearly demarcate a self from a world. To the contrary, the circle of which Derrida is speaking is the mind's passage through worldly concerns, through an interest in everyday and at times meaningless, nonsensical affairs, in order to constitute itself by returning to itself, regaining itself after having momentarily lost itself. Thinking is a calling of the self forward into the world, into worldly engagement and interest; it is not only serious introspective self-scrutiny, much less calculative rationality. The difference or the boundary between the seriousness of philosophical or of scientific reflection and the meanderings of everyday private nonsense is therefore, as far as deconstruction—and, of course, psychoanalysis—is concerned, not as clearly marked off as we are generally led to believe.

Rather than being something deconstruction and psychoanalysis coincidentally happen to share in common, this is the trace of Derrida's acknowledged debt to Freud and of deconstruction as a reflection on the meaning of Freudian practice rather than as an effort merely to extend Freudian theory. The image of thinking that Derrida puts forth is deeply indebted to a Freudian thematics of free association and evenly hovering or freely floating attention. His efforts at times to stage this image of thought performatively in his writings has resulted in a tremendous backlash of hostility from critics, despite the fact that his more stylistically experimental texts are rather minor in number as compared to the rigorous academic approach of his early period and the more conversational, conventionally philosophical approach of his work in the last two decades of his publishing. Derrida's writing has frustrated critics much in the same way that psychoanalysis tends to frustrate the demands of today's consumers of mental health services. For both patients and insurance agents who demand the production of "results" quickly and unambiguously, and who often imagine that psychoanalysis is about relentlessly trying to understand the truth about one's past, a properly Freudian practice as an effort to abandon precisely this demand and to recover an experience of mind as something other than a producer of self-knowledge can appear intolerable.

When Derrida writes, "The mind is what it is, says what it means, only *by returning*," (1987, p. 26; emphases in original), he is describing a model of mind as neither a subject nor an object but as an open, ecstatic process. This process is what the mind actively-passively *is*, and in a way that continuously or repetitively loses itself, abandons itself to the world in which it is constitutively immersed and that it will never be able to think absolutely in the mode of objective self-presence as some formal, stable or ideal abstraction. The metaphysical fantasy of a self capable of standing objectively over and above the world was always nothing but that— a fantasy—and yet a particularly powerful and tenacious fantasy. What Derrida describes as a movement by means of which the self becomes itself in returning to itself, from the beginning and before its appearing to itself as self-presence, describes the self not as an object but as an auto-affective process. This would not be the solipsistic event of a self reflecting itself into itself, pursuing a "depth psychology" of personal and inward journey towards truth, but an ecstatic movement beyond itself, repetitively venturing into and returning from an environment that is inherently foreign, strange, unpredictable and therefore anxiety-provoking. A mind that loses itself yet that rediscovers itself in its capacity to return to itself is a mind defined by its capacity to *individuate* itself, not by its capacity to self-reflect so as to accumulate self-knowledge and self-understanding.[4]

The parergonal frame would thus be the repository of a mind that is constitutively unmindful in its operation, as the trace of a mind that must forget itself in order to return to itself in an act of memorization that is also a necessary passage through the world and through practices of material, technical inscription (*writing*, in Derrida's expanded sense). This is what situates the work of deconstruction, "*Between* the outside and inside, between the external and the internal edge-line, the framer and the framed, the figure and the ground, form and content, signifier and signified, and *so on* for any two-faced opposition. The trait thus divides in this place where it takes place." (1987, p. 12; emphases in original). The trait, edge, or frame that divides mind and environment, like that between art and life or,

**52** The spectrality of the clinical frame

following Milner, the symbolic reality of psychoanalysis and the ordinary reality of everyday affairs, does so not by imposing a strict and substantial boundary subject to calculable rules and regulations, but by dividing the worlds so demarcated and differentiated *from themselves* by putting each at play and at risk by relating them irreducibly and experimentally (unpredictably) to one another. What relates mind and world in this way, like the *work* of art which cannot be reduced to an industrial model of production, would be a "framed gap" or "temporal spatial frame" that separates and distinguishes, that organizes and that circulates differences, and that is not itself a work but that puts to work a difference that makes something like mind, like art, like therapeutic transformation via the clinical work of interpretation possible.

The frame as Derrida conceives of it then, like Milner's framed gap that both separates and distinguishes, that *marks off* in a way that makes it something less than a work but that puts to work a certain difference that makes clinical work possible, would therefore be both a part of the work of art or of analysis and something essentially inert, something that retreats into the background, concealing itself in order to be able to function, to create difference. This is why Derrida is able to write, "*There is* frame, but the frame *does not exist*" (1987, p. 81; emphases in original). This apparently nonsensical statement expresses what Milner was attempting to describe in terms of a frame that is not an object in the ordinary sense, something composed of "temporal space." A "framed gap" does not properly exist as an object; it is *there* in its non-being or its non-existence as what marks the difference between existence and non-existence or between "two realities" without belonging stably to either category. The frame is an instance of that which supplementarily derives from, but in such a way as to constitute, the creative illusion of the transference from which the possibility of profound and lasting therapeutic transformation emerges. Accounting for this possibility is difficult because what it describes is fragile in that it resists representation while making representation not only possible but compelling, to the point of intoxication for the artist, as well as for anyone who appreciates art to the point of being actively inspired by works of art—those without the capacity for remaining merely passive consumers of marketable artistic products. The passion for art too is a part of the *work* of art, which is to say a part of the process of individuation that art, like psychoanalysis, both supports and cultivates. Derrida indicates as much when he asks, "How could a circle place itself *en abyme*?" (1987, p. 24). This was Derrida's way, at the time, of posing the question as to the relationship between the frame and the work. This is a question that psychoanalysis today is in danger of forgetting, to the detriment of its own continued relevance in the saturated marketplace of contemporary therapeutic techniques.

## José Bleger: the institutional ghost world of the pre-transferential fund

The English-speaking analytic world has recently begun to discover the work of the Argentinian theorist José Bleger. Particular attention has been devoted to

The spectrality of the clinical frame **53**

Bleger's important essay, "Psycho-Analysis of the Psycho-Analytic Frame" (1967).[5] More than any other author who has written about the clinical analytic frame, Bleger develops the most sophisticated and challenging insights originally offered by Milner in determining the concept, and that, as I have tried to show, anticipate crucial aspects of what would become deconstruction. Even more than Milner, Bleger's essay communicates explicitly with key themes in Derrida's writing—in particular the theme of "spectrality," which Bleger thinks in terms of the "ghost world" of the clinic—to such an extent that one is tempted to wonder if Bleger was not reading and being influenced directly by Derrida. This suspicion is quickly dispelled when one recalls that the date of the essay's original presentation at the Second Argentine Psychoanalytic Congress in Buenos Aires in 1966 precedes not only Derrida's international reputation but even his reputation in France (it would not be until 1967 that the publication of three volumes—*Speech and Phenomena* [1973], *Of Grammatology* [1976] and *Writing and Difference* [1978]—would indicate the originality and broad relevance of Derrida's project), and it appeared decades before any explicit elaboration of an organized theory of the spectral in Derrida's writing. One can only imagine what might have occurred had Bleger not died at such a tragically young age (of a heart attack at forty-nine) and if the two thinkers had encountered one another's work directly.

In her appreciation of Bleger's contributions Haydée Faimberg (2012) writes, "The exploration of contradiction is at the very heart of José Bleger's dialectical thinking" (p. 983). While I agree that the elaboration of contradiction or, perhaps more accurately, paradox is essential to Bleger's talent as a thinker and as a writer (he considered himself first and foremost a dialectical materialist), what is more original and creative in Bleger's thinking is that he often treats contradiction or paradox in a non-dialectical or post-classical way. That is, rather than seeking to overcome or to resolve contradictions in the service of integration and shared, mutual identity, Bleger more often than not insists on logics that sustain the positive effects of conflict, paradox and difference. This puts him in closer proximity to the anti-dialectical, deconstructive projects of Nietzsche, Heidegger and Derrida. Despite the fact that Bleger and Derrida were most certainly completely unfamiliar with each others' contributions, this does not preclude the possibility that the Argentinian psychoanalyst actively haunts the margins of the discourse of deconstruction.

Situating Bleger's 1967 essay beyond a classical dialectical logic is recommended by nothing less than the title of the essay itself. In attempting to provide a "psychoanalysis of the psycho-analytic frame" Bleger indicates from the very outset that thinking through the problems we face in accounting for the clinical frame will require that we think in a manner that is contradictory and paradoxical. The title announces that what follows will not be simply a theory of the analytic frame. Bleger is stating quite clearly that thinking about the psychoanalytic frame invites psychoanalysis to a certain *mise-en-abyme,* which is to say a situation in which the reflective subject and the object of reflection cannot be approached as formally extrinsic to one another, as in dialectics. There is something about thinking the frame in analysis that confounds classical thinking, and that requires

**54** The spectrality of the clinical frame

a "psychoanalytic" approach—that is, an approach that tends to what necessarily remains concealed or unconscious in the effort at theorizing itself—to thinking about the structural conditions that make the psychoanalytic clinic (i.e. mutative interpretation as a therapeutic practice) possible. Bleger invites us to consider the conditions of possibility of an interpretive clinical relationship, and he indicates that this cannot be achieved from an abstract theoretical position outside psychoanalysis as an experiential, therapeutic procedure. A psychoanalysis of the psychoanalytic frame will thus involve a thinking about what psychoanalysis necessarily finds difficult to think about because it makes something like psychoanalysis possible in the first place. This situation cannot be resolved dialectically without losing its orientation.

At no point does Bleger make mention of Marion Milner, but he does open with reference to Winnicott's notion of the "setting," which he recasts in terms of the "psychoanalytic situation" as the clinical relationship in its entirety, and in terms of which he distinguishes between the analytic process and the analytic frame, which he calls a "non-process" (p. 511). The distinction here is that between the analytic process as something that by definition evolves, and the frame as that which must remain stable. In that it remains relatively stable, however, this does not mean that the frame is somehow atemporal, that it is not in its own unusual way processive. Rather the question is that of the difference—and this is the subtle paradox that the opening paragraphs of the essay struggle with and to which the author will repeatedly return—between a process that is clearly temporal, in that its ongoing nature essentially involves change, and a process that also implicates time in an essential way but that appears as a "non-process" to the extent that it must conceal its temporality and appear absolutely unchanging and stable (in what Bleger calls an "ideal" clinical situation). This is why Bleger puts "non-process" under quotation marks and goes on to qualify that the frame is a non-process "in the sense that it is made up of *constants* within whose *bounds* the [analytic] process takes place" (ibid.; emphasis added). The frame as a "non-process" is very much processive, very much temporal, but in a way that is composed of *constants*—in contrast to the analytic process as composed of *variables*—whose function is to give to the well-maintained frame the power of *binding*.

What is bound by the frame consists, as always, of a group of heterogenous elements: "Thus we include within the psycho-analytic frame the role of the analyst, the set of space (atmosphere) and time factors, and part of the technique (including problems concerning the fixing and keeping of times, fees, interruptions, etc.)" (ibid.). As anyone who attempts to define the strict nature and boundaries of the notion of the frame encounters, we are dealing with something that is undecidably both extremely general and intensely specific. This is compounded by the question as to whether these aspects of the frame are to be thought of as contained inside the frame or whether they do not rather constitute the frame itself. Are these aspects of the clinical relationship a part of the relationship as delimited or marked off by the frame, or are they the very marks that constitute the frame itself as something that lies clearly outside the analytic process as a "non-process" to which the work of

The spectrality of the clinical frame  **55**

analysis would stand opposed? Bleger seems to be refining the question that Milner had implicitly encountered in having originally addressed the frame as a "framed gap" or "temporal space": In dividing the reality "inside" the analysis from the reality "outside" the analysis, what is the status of the frame itself and on which side of the divide should its borders be located? Are the components of the frame inside or outside the frame which makes the process possible, or do they compose the frame itself and therefore should they not be considered a proper part of the analytic work? Bleger's brilliant move will be to demonstrate that these are not specious or abstruse questions, rather they are crucial issues for any attempt to think rigorously about the nature of the clinical efficacy of psychoanalysis: "The problem I want to look into concerns those analyses in which the frame is not a problem— *precisely to show that it is a problem*" (p. 511; emphasis added).

The invariably maintained frame eludes description as either an object or a process—hence a "non-process," which does not name something other than a process (i.e. an object) but a process that dissimulates its processive nature, a process that is still not an object but that obviates the opposition between object and process, a "non-process" that could also be a "non-object." Bleger writes, "while it exists as such it seems to be non-existent" (p. 512). The existence of the frame is defined not by its appearance but by its effectiveness; its effectiveness is threatened the moment its appearance constitutes a horizon. Disappearing at the very moment that it threatens to appear, the frame belongs to a dimension that Bleger calls "the most primitive and undifferentiated organization"—a domain of "ultra-things" that is at once a "ghost world." This primitive organization is not lost because it is repressed or hidden. It is present to the very extent that it appears as if it were not there, and if it actually were not there nothing else would appear as it is: "It is what remains implicit but on which the explicit depends" (ibid.).

Importantly, and in contrast to a much heralded concept in the contemporary psychoanalytic literature, what Bleger is describing does not constitute a third domain that is added to a pre-existing two. The ghost world of the frame is not the "analytic third" as something allegedly "co-constructed" in the relationship between patient and analyst. Bleger is describing what allows the psychoanalytic domain—what Milner had called "the special kind of reality of a psychoanalytic session"—to appear in its difference from the ordinary world outside the clinic. He writes, "what we do not perceive is also present. And precisely because of this, that 'ghost world' is also present in the frame even when this has not been broken" (p. 512). Straining the bounds of classical logic, he is describing how the frame, as what exists in appearing to be non-existent, cannot be simply present when it is not perceivable. As a "most primitive and undifferentiated organization" that cannot be described in terms of a classically metaphysical opposition between presence and absence, the frame is not something newly created by a previously existing intersubjective relationship. Instead the frame as a structure of repetition discloses what is *there* in a way that precedes and that makes possible the opposition of perception and intelligibility, or of reality and interpretation. The "presence" of this ghost world can be neither *fully* perceived nor *fully* understood; it only appears at

**56** The spectrality of the clinical frame

the moment it withdraws or when the illusion of its existence is broken, and this is precisely what constitutes its "ghostly" character.

This is why Bleger, in what is perhaps the boldest claim he makes about this ghost world that defies description with regard to basic categories that define our notion of objectivity (presence *or* absence, time *or* space, etc.), writes, "Summing up, one might say that the frame (thus defined as a problem) is the most perfect repetition compulsion"—perfect as a form of repetition, but one that also remains a problem in that it conceals its status as repetition and presents itself as a constant, as if a process were not occurring—"and that actually there are two frames, one which is suggested and kept up by the analyst, and consciously accepted by the patient, and the other, that of the 'ghost world,' on which the patient projects" (pp. 512–513).

Here it is as if, at the very moment that Bleger manages to provide a description of this strange existential status of the frame as constitutively in excess of or as other than itself, as something that cannot merely be designated or pointed to, that suddenly he begins talking about "two frames"—one that the analyst maintains and one that the patient brings. In the same way that it no sooner appears than it withdraws, no sooner is it defined than it doubles. This is why Bleger asserts the ontological or existential claim that, "Each frame *is*, and does not admit ambiguity" (p. 514; emphasis in original), by which he means that each individual analytic process is possessed of its own singularity and does not admit itself as an instance of some universal category. Where there are two frames, interpretation consists in differentiating or opening up the difference between them, not in exposing or explaining some concealed psychological content. Tending to the frame has nothing to do with interpreting unconscious fantasy or defense but with interpretation as a process of differentiating difference—of repeatedly *marking* the difference between "two realities" or "two frames" or in whatever form this *differance* appears.

When he emphasized the frame as a "non-process"—as that which remains constant and invariable over time, in contrast to the clinical dialogue—it seemed as if Bleger was speaking against Milner's conception of the frame as stable like an object occupying space but essentially temporal, as a "temporal spatial frame." Bleger proceeds by emphasizing (initially, at least) the stable, "spatial" aspects of the frame, whereas Milner is drawn to emphasize its temporal openness. Both, however, are each in their own way highlighting complementary aspects of the clinical frame that can neither be divorced from one another nor (dialectically) collapsed into a simple unity. This dynamic economy of spatial and temporal metaphors in both authors' attempts to grapple with the status of the clinical frame recalls what I had demonstrated in Chapter 1 with regard to the work of Winnicott and Ogden: something is operating in these texts or in these efforts to submit clinical experience to theoretical representation that resists formal description and that requires the mobilization of complex metaphorical frameworks relating space and time in order to capture a counterintuitive yet irreducible dimension of psychoanalytic clinical experience, one defined by the becoming-time of space, the becoming-space of time.

The spectrality of the clinical frame **57**

As if attempting to arrest a conceptual instability that begins to make itself felt from the outset, Bleger writes, "The frame refers to a strategy rather than to a technique" (p. 511). This statement raises more questions than it provides clarification. What exactly is the difference between a "strategy" (*una estrategia*) and a "technique" (*la técnica*), and is this distinction any more or less absolute as it pertains to psychoanalysis than to anything else? If we were to speculate as to what Bleger might be attempting to get at here, we might proceed by assuming that by "strategy" is intended something rather more open and flexible than the more mechanically oriented word "technique." A strategy would seem to imply that not everything is predetermined, that we are in large part relying on our wits as we proceed, whereas a technique would seem to imply something that is already fixed, a procedure worked out in advance and that would be universally applicable with every patient and regardless as to the singularity of the case.

If this is indeed what Bleger means then the following must be noted: first, no sooner has he emphasized the stable, "spatial" aspect of the frame than he is already deferring to its more open, flexible qualities (like Milner in the shift from the framed gap to the temporal spatial frame). Second, when has psychoanalytic "technique" ever meant anything more than a "strategy" in this open, flexible sense? Unlike manualized therapeutic procedures—like hypnosis, which Freud had rejected in elaborating an analytic approach, and like the variety of cognitive, behavioral and pharmaceutical approaches that claim today to have superseded psychoanalysis but that in fact return us to the dream of a single technique that objectively works for everyone—psychoanalytic "technique" never indicated a purely mechanical, universal procedure.[6] Third, in contrast to the absence of any formal rules concerning what occurs and how the analyst is to proceed in the analytic process, if there is anything about the analytic situation that is technically, universally formalizable it would seem to be the frame itself, which is presumably why Bleger begins by describing it initially as a "non-process."

What I am attempting to indicate is that these are not illogical contradictions in the author's thinking but non-logical paradoxes inherent to the phenomenon that he is trying to describe. This undecidable, oscillating logic between the frame's being temporal or spatial, open or closed, playful or technical is at work on so many levels and from the very beginning of the essay. We might extend our recognition of the persistence of this dilemma to cover other debates in the professional field such as those surrounding the difference between the mutative values of interpretation versus empathy, of the primacy of the drive or the object, or over whether psychoanalysis is a "one-person" or a "two-person" psychology. All such debates, as Derrida encourages us to appreciate, are predicated on the assumption that the difference between what is open and what is closed can ever be figured as a formal, absolute opposition. Such oppositions are always only provisional, inscribed historically in local, evolving contexts. According to the procedures of deconstruction—which, like those of psychoanalysis, are always only strategic and playful—what appears formalizable according to the logic and structure of opposition is inevitably revealed to be coordinated in differ*a*nce. As we will see in the next two chapters,

**58** The spectrality of the clinical frame

the most trenchant form that this opposition has historically assumed and that threatens us most today if it is not thought critically is the opposition between the human and the technical, as a version of the opposition of openness and closure that Winnicott, Milner and Bleger all give us to believe is in no way tenable in the context of the psychoanalytic clinic.

The clinical frame thus manifests something that is both stable *and* open, both structured *and* unstructured, spatial *and* temporal in ways that do not conform to any reliable oppositions between such terms or that would leave them uncontaminated and kept each in their proper place. This is why thinking the temporal spatial, processive non-process that is the analytic frame requires something like a psychoanalysis of psychoanalysis. Reflecting on what distinguishes the analytic relationship or rather the symbolic clinical reality from the ordinary reality outside the consulting room requires that psychoanalysis be placed *en abyme*, as a mirror placed before another mirror.

As Bleger indicates, this is not the case when we attempt to think about breakdowns in the maintenance of the analytic frame and about the consequences that generally follow, which is what most of the literature on the frame concerns itself with, and not without good reason. Bleger states unequivocally that this is what he is not interested in, that he is interested instead in what occurs in an "ideal analysis" where no such breakdown occurs, about the status and nature of the frame *"when it is not a problem"* (p. 511; emphasis in original)—that is, when the frame *works*. When a strong clinical frame is being maintained and an analytic process is occurring, why indeed would one wish to pay any attention to it so as to call it into question? Drawing the patient's attention to and attempting to analyze a functional frame can only be experienced as a disruption. Why would one want to analyze what makes analysis possible in the first place, and why would doing so be experienced as threatening? Why, as Bleger insists, is the frame a problem precisely when it is not a problem?

There are superficially obvious, pragmatic answers to these questions, and it would be easy to read Bleger as if he were simply indicating that an analysis of the frame be attempted only at the conclusion of a very thorough and successful analysis. It does not seem to me that this is what he is getting at. Bleger appears concerned less with establishing rules for when to interpret the frame and when not to do so—a gesture that would be in keeping with efforts to regulate the temporal space of the clinic managerially—than he is with expanding the very concept of interpretation itself.

The distinction Bleger draws between the operative frame which is concealed to the extent that it retreats into the background as an enduring analytic process occurs, and the frame as it comes to the fore in the midst of disruption, breakdown and enactment, recalls Heidegger's distinction in *Being and Time* between *Zuhandenheit* and *Vorhandenheit*—translated as "handiness" and "objective presence."[7] Heidegger's (1996, pp. 64–65) privileged example in distinguishing these two existential modalities is the hammer (a technological artifact, wielded by the hand). In an everyday sense, the hammer exists in a way that is not the object of my reflection. Should I need a hammer I know that it is there for me and I know how to use it, but this is not conscious, reflective knowledge—the hammer is simply *there*, I need not think "about" it. When I need the hammer to accomplish a given task I retrieve it and do what I need to do with it in an apparently mechanical and mindless way. I do not consciously reflect on the hammer and rehearse procedures of hammering in my mind before performing the task *at hand*. In other words, the hammer is the repository of a knowledge that is not theoretical knowledge, a pre-reflective knowledge that the subject does not need to represent to itself in advance of carrying out its intended task. Such pre-theoretical, pre-representational knowledge is not knowledge I have in the form of information stored "in" my mind; rather it is manifest in the ways I comport myself in the world, as in the relationship between hand and hammer and the inevitable gestures that their conjunctions realize.

Should I reach for the hammer and find it broken, however, now I am confronted by the hammer in isolation and as such, as torn out of what Heidegger calls its "context of relevance." Now I am forced to think about it and to see that it will not work, which is to say that it is no longer a hammer in an ordinary sense that otherwise need not be thought about or tended to. The broken hammer is objectively present—I encounter it in the meaninglessness of its singularity when it no longer functions in its ordinary manner and context. As objectively present the hammer is an *object* in the purest sense: something essentially unrelated to anything else, something independent because it is without use value and without meaning.

Heidegger's point in preparing this analysis is to demonstrate that the conscious, theoretical knowledge pursued by science and philosophy is always predicated on a more generalized, practical knowledge that discloses the ways in which we always already find ourselves "in-the-world" (the hyphens are there again to indicate that this "in" is not the ordinary spatial sense of "in," and that our relationship with the world is again not one of mere spatial occupancy). This is the existential, factical domain that Heidegger's analysis is oriented towards disclosing because it is precisely that which is covered over at the level of everyday affairs, and which is intrinsically repudiated by the relentless pursuit of positivist knowledge. This only occurs to the extent that science remains a figure of metaphysics as that which promises the programmability of conscious self-reflection and of objective presence. This is the promise upon which are built all contemporary industries of advertising, marketing and human resources.

Not incidentally, in attempting to account for the phenomena of the ghost world of the clinical frame, Bleger references the "factical" orientation of "the existentialists" (p. 516). He describes a "factic ego" that is an "ego of belonging," which is also a "non-ego of the frame" and which "includes the body" (p. 513)—a "non-ego" that is at once a "meta-ego" (p. 517). In that "it is the body-space and body-setting non-differentiation" (p. 517), the frame is not something "inside" of which this non-ego subsists. Instead the frame is continuous with this aspect of mind itself, in a way that cannot be grasped by a thinking that continues to insist on absolute distinctions between subjects and objects, time and space, body and

**60** The spectrality of the clinical frame

world: "The frame is the most primitive part of the personality, it is the fusion ego-body-world" (p. 514).

Bleger is attempting to depict in the vocabulary of psychoanalysis what Heidegger had called *Da-sein*: the way human beings are irreducibly in-the-world as *there* in the sense of our experiencing the world first and foremost as meaningful, and not in a psychological but in an ontological way (even if we are not possessed of an ideological explanation of some meaning of life, we are still capable of experiencing life as meaning*ful*). That he includes within his analysis questions about the body (as one might expect from a psychoanalyst) distances Bleger from Heidegger but puts him in direct proximity to Derrida whose effort to describe a form of material inscription (writing) beyond the opposition of presence and absence was always guided by a Heideggerian reading of Freud, and by a Freudian reading of Heidegger—readings that intend to focus on proximal zones of intermediacy between subjects and objects, presence and absence, body and mind, matter and spirit. It is thus no accident then that both Derrida and Bleger wind up talking about *ghosts* and in terms of a general thematics of spectrality: frame, repetition, double, present-absent space-time.

In *Specters of Marx* (1994), Derrida cast the theme of differantial space-time in terms of a thinking about ghosts as a way of posing questions about our relationships with the collective and historical past. This was in order to retrieve the question of memory as what had initially united the concerns of Nietzsche, Freud and Heidegger, which is to say of both deconstruction and psychoanalysis. Writing about haunting as repetition and as return of what was never there but that is not simply absent—an intermediary, transitional space between life and death, in which the boundaries between past and present, memory and perception are destabilized—was Derrida's later conceptual refinement of what had always been the province of deconstruction. In this text in particular he links this concern to a question that is also central to Bleger, both in "Psycho-analysis of the psycho-analytic frame" and elsewhere: the question of our relationship to institutions. "A relationship which lasts for years," Bleger writes, referring to the clinical frame, "in which a set of norms and attitudes is kept up, is nothing less than a true definition of *institution*" (pp. 511–512; emphasis in original). For Derrida, the question of our relationship to institutions is the question of inheritance, of the active-passive, transitional relation to the other: "Inheritance is never a *given*, it is always a task" (1994, p. 54; emphasis in original). Can we say that the task of an analysis is for the patient to inherit his or her own past through the intermediary institution of the frame, or through the technology of the analyst's unconscious as this is inscribed both by and *as* the frame? Perhaps this is why the frame must be *held* and not explicitly discussed or theoretically, consciously dismantled. Is holding the frame more like holding a hammer or more like holding an infant? Or does it rather indicate a strange zone of overlap between these gestures and between these different types of objects? Would the pre-reflective clinical technique that actively-passively *is* the spectral ghost world of the frame be what underwrites a practice like analytic neutrality, which so

The spectrality of the clinical frame **61**

many patients experience as threatening because it evokes an experience of an other who at times seems to be "not really there"?

By remaining neutral and maintaining a reliably stable frame—one that constitutes "the most perfect repetition compulsion" because again it repeats difference so reliably that it seems as if nothing is changing, making possible more profound changes than are ordinarily accessible—the analytic frame*work* merges with the framework that the patient brings to the treatment and which determines the background or "institutional" form of all of his or her underlying interpersonal relationships. For Derrida, it is precisely this concern with the spectral materiality of structures and traditions of inheritance that makes deconstruction, Marxism and psychoanalysis more than mere academic schools, something that makes these disciplines capable, as per Marx's famous eleventh thesis on Feuerbach, of changing the world rather than merely interpreting it, and yet strangely capable of producing material change through practices of interpretation:

> It is because deconstruction interferes with solid structures, "material" institutions, and not only with discourses or signifying representations, that it is always distinct from an analysis or "critique." And in order to be pertinent, deconstruction works as strictly as possible in that place where the supposedly "internal" order of the philosophical is articulated by (internal *and* external) necessity with the institutional conditions and forms of teaching. To the point where the concept of institution itself would be subjected to the same deconstructive treatment.
>
> (Derrida 1987, pp. 19–20; emphasis in original)

For Bleger, "each institution is a portion of the individual's personality" (p. 512), which is to say that it is artificial to speak of some absolute demarcation between a subject and the institutions to which he or she belongs. Institutions are the setting of our social existence, and much like the psychoanalytic setting they are experienced as somehow in between the human and the technological, the living and the dead. There would be no human relationships to speak of without institutionalized (in Derridean terms: archival) repositories of inheritance that form the basis for history and tradition, whether this occurs at the collective socio-political level or at the most intimate level as in the psychoanalytic clinic. What is important to both Derrida and Bleger is that in order to function, in order to support and to cultivate human relatedness, institutional frameworks or technologies must be preserved or cared for in their background status, as neither objectively present nor objectively absent, but as undecidably beyond or before the structures that encourage us to oppose subjectivity and objectivity, presence and absence. "In the same way we speak of the 'ghost member,'" Bleger writes:

> we must accept that institutions and the frame *always* make up a "ghost world," that of the most primitive and undifferentiated organization… The knowledge of something is only apparent in the absence of that something,

**62** The spectrality of the clinical frame

until it is incorporated as an internal object. But what we do not perceive is also present. And precisely because of this, that "ghost world" is also present in the frame even when this has not been broken.

(1967, p. 512; emphasis in original)

The temptation here is quickly to assimilate what Bleger means by a "ghost world" to a thinking about the transference, as if he meant that past relationships haunt us even when—especially when—they are not recognized as belonging to the past but are conflated with the present. On closer inspection it becomes clear that this is not all that Bleger has in mind. In thinking about a ghost world as he describes it, emphasis must be put equally on the "ghost" part—the object or object relationship that repeats and that returns from the past in the present, the difference between past and present remaining nonetheless objectively intact—as on the "world" part, as a "most primitive and undifferentiated organization" prior to any distinctions between a subject and its objects, which is not to say prior to any difference whatsoever. Bleger's concept of the ghost world is not as an objectively present world full of ghosts that repeats the past in the present but as a ghostly world whose status is itself spectral or liminal, in between present and past, neither one nor the other but functioning always in the background as a link between the two. To analyze this ghost world would not be to empty it of its content or to dispel it away but to hold it in such a way that facilitates its doubling or its becoming other than itself. Holding the frame means interpreting the frame by allowing the frame to differentiate itself, in terms of the "two frames" according to Bleger, or the "two realities" as described by Milner.

In speaking about the frame in this way, Bleger is not saying that the frame is where the the patient's intimate personal past makes itself most felt in the intersubjective, relational present. He is talking about the frame *as* frame—as *institution* and therefore as something non-human, technical—and as belonging to a dimension of clinical experience in which sharp distinctions between past and present cannot be made (quite unlike in the dialectical interpretation of the transference). The "most primitive and undifferentiated organization" that Bleger portrays is prior to the differentiation of past from present, prior to the differentiation of subject and object. The frame as a site of "symbiosis" (p. 512; see also Churcher and Bleger 2013) is primitive and undifferentiated not merely in the sense that it is developmentally early, but in the sense that basic distinctions and oppositions that structure the ordinary relationship between mind and world are only nascent and not yet fully operative. The frame is "primitive and undifferentiated" not merely in the sense of its being infantile but in the sense of its being radically "experience near," and in a way that is disruptive and anxiety-provoking the closer we get to it.

The uniqueness of Bleger's contribution thus lies in its concern not so much with the contents of this ghost world as with its spectral, ghostly status as neither present nor past, neither present nor absent. The frame does not reflect a past present prior to the present present of the treatment. This is what the transference reflects. The frame rather manifests—or, we might say, recalling Milner and Derrida,

The spectrality of the clinical frame **63**

that it *marks*, inscribes—something prior to the absolute distinction between past and present, a past that was never present, an intermediary zone both between *and* before presence and absence. The encroachment of spatial metaphors here is crucial, and it likely informs Bleger's choice of the term ghost *world* (*mundo fantasma*) as suggestive of something both spatial and temporal, as defined by the conjunction of space and time and as insisting prior to their distinction, to which Heidegger had brought attention. The frame is spectral or ghostly in that it is *there* in not being "there" in the ordinary metaphysical sense of objective presence. When it is called to appear as objectively present the ghost world of the frame disappears and we are confronted with the impossibility of its full presence. Drawing attention to it makes it go away, until the next time, when it comes back.

This is why Bleger writes, "The frame is maintained and tends to be maintained (actively, by the psycho-analyst) as invariable; and while it exists as such it seems to be non-existent" (p. 512). Recall that for Derrida, "*There is* frame, but the frame *does not exist*" (1987, p. 81; emphases in original). The frame does not exist as an object in objective presence; it is *there* (*Da*) but not in an ordinary sense according to which we think space, time and matter (as that which occupies space and time, and as what is objectively present). It is not simply that the analyst cannot get the patient to think about the frame without causing disruption, provoking anxiety by causing the presence of the frame to become absent. Rather, the frame instantiates something that cannot be thought "about" in a classical sense, in that it resists representation such that efforts to represent or to analyze it in a classical manner move us away from it as an experience towards abstraction. The ghost world is one in which symbolization works in reverse, creating distance and uncanniness rather than proximity and familiarity. The frame cannot be thought about abstractly in an ordinary, representational sense; rather it must be *held* in a way that exceeds the ordinary oppositions of thought and practice, memory and perception. This non-representability does not reflect a limit intrinsic to the human mind, it is an aspect of the differantial spectrality of the temporal spatial frame itself. Bleger calls this the "dumbness" (1967, p. 517) of the frame, which he finds "peculiar" in that it resists being described directly without losing the quality he intends to capture. This is also what prevents psychoanalysis from becoming a calculable, manualized form of treatment.

## Resonance, opening, tradition

For Derrida this loss in representation is irreducible; it is not a failure of conceptual thinking but the insistence of something that essentially determines but that seems outside or incommensurable with conceptual, representational logic. As we saw in Chapter 1, it is this loss of meaning that the undecidability of the "concept" ("neither word nor concept") of differance intends to affirm. This affirmation is what is repeated when we *work on* texts by Freud, by Derrida, by Marion Milner and José Bleger, by those who the overwhelmingly vast majority of us will never have known as part of our individual pasts, but who will *live on* in and through us by

**64** The spectrality of the clinical frame

means of an inheritance that projects itself forward as a tradition, and that does so by means of the *binding* power of institutional technologies that are strangely capable of relating us to and that bring to life a seemingly dead past that was at no point ever a part of our own experience of the living present.

This is also, at the same time—which is *never* the *same* time—what we work on when we work on ourselves in the process of a psychoanalysis. This work is undertaken by the patient and the analyst alike, each in their own time, in their own individuating temporalities which are both constitutively out of joint and yet synchronized—or rather diachronized, because analysis is never an effort at collapsing differences—by the frame, by means of which the participants are able to individuate themselves through such an intimate encounter with one another. Winnicott described precisely this when he wrote: "Although healthy persons communicate and enjoy communicating, the other fact is equally true, that *each individual is an isolate, permanently non-communicating, permanently unknown, in fact, unfound* ... At the centre of each human being is an incommunicado element, and this is sacred and most worthy of preservation" (1965, p. 187; emphasis in original). As sacred this center is spectral, which is what it means to say that as center it is "unfound," as radically dis-placed or in de-fault. If this center were merely absent, neither cultivated nor preserved, one would not be dealing with an individual in any meaningful sense of the word.

Hans Loewald, in a text that records the traces of his debt to Heidegger, who is not acknowledged explicitly in that text but who haunts it rather intensively, speaks of this diachronic function of the clinical relationship in terms that it is possible to discover traces of elsewhere across the analytic literature (as the next chapter will demonstrate), but which has yet to be systematized into a coherent discourse. In his essay on *Sublimation* (1988), Loewald too invokes a spectral vocabulary, one of "twilight valences" (p. 59), of "closeness-in-distance" (p. 58) and of "waves, oscillations, vibrations in a magnetic field" (p. 25). Loewald's primary concern in that text is to provide an account of symbolization in terms of "non-climactic processes"—a reference to Winnicott, but also to Freud, and inadvertently to Bleger's concept of the clinical frame as institution. To this end he speaks out against a classical thinking in terms of subjects and objects (yet without invoking the term metaphysics), and in favor of a revised concept of primary narcissism as the site of, "Differentiating processes... conceptualized as primary internalizations and externalizations" (p. 17). In one of the essay's most penetrating and suggestive passages he writes:

> We are far from adequately understanding the pleasure in higher organization and the unpleasure in less or lower organization. Part of the difficulty seems to be the fact that theorists in this area are preoccupied with quantitative factors and consequently neglect phenomena of *resonance* in favor of data on input and output of energy quanta. "Stimulation" should not be conceived exclusively as increase of the quantity of excitation; in many instances it can be thought of as resonance with the "wave length" of a neighboring system. Stimulation can result from an openness to the latter's level of binding

or organization of activity. The neighboring system, in the case of such hypercathexis is simultaneously open to, in tune with, the "receiving" system. Stimulation, in such resonance, would consist in qualitative change of some kind: the organization of the degree of tension preexisting in the receiving system is changed. As Freud said of the qualitative characteristic in pleasure and unpleasure, so is resonance a phenomenon implicated with rhythm, with time, in ways that are not clear.

(1988, p. 32; emphasis in original)

*Resonance* is a word possessed of tremendous import, both philosophically and psychoanalytically. It was a word used by Heidegger while working privately on the *Beïtrage zur Philosophie (Vom Ereignis)*, which is generally considered to represent the "turn" in Heidegger's thinking away from the existential approach of *Being and Time* and toward the question of the relationship between the human and technology. This was the period from 1936 to 1938, although this text would not be made available publicly until 1989, one year after the publication of Loewald's essay on sublimation. "Resonance," says Loewald in this passage, is "a phenomenon implicated with rhythm, with time, in ways that are not clear." One wonders if Loewald is not withholding something essential here, as although it could never pretend to become absolutely clear or conceptually transparent, the conjunction of resonance with rhythm and time would have been far more clear to a student of Heidegger than to psychoanalysts.

Derridean differ*a*nce, which operates spectrally as announced in the middle voice, as neither passive nor active, and as neither substantive nor event ("No more is resonance the act of resonating" [Derrida 1982, p. 9]), would itself be graspable only dimly and in an ungovernable way, as irreducibly implicated with rhythm and with time, the traces of which can nevertheless be read *virtually* everywhere. "Always differing and deferring," wrote Derrida, "the trace is never as it is in the presentation of itself. It erases itself in presenting itself, muffles itself in resonating, like the *a* of writing itself, inscribing its pyramid in differ*a*nce" (1982, p. 23). Quite strikingly, but according to a pattern that becomes increasingly difficult to attribute to pure chance, Loewald opens his theory of symbolism with the following example:

> I begin with one example of symbolization. In writing down (or voicing) my thoughts I give them visibility (or sound) in the form of symbols. Through my sensory-motor acts of writing, and reading what I wrote, the flow of my thinking acquires a materiality, a presence it did not have before. The words and sentences I write and see before me represent my thoughts in the form of visible symbols. Thus, these thoughts—immaterial insofar as I cannot apprehend them with my senses—materialize for me, and in materializing they gain distance from me and become elements of the world around me. They are "communicated" to me myself by these sensory-motor acts and can be communicated to others. I do not invent or construct material signs for my thoughts de novo, as I do when I draw a short line and decree that it shall

**66** The spectrality of the clinical frame

signify the idea "horse." Words and sentences are embedded in a linguistic tradition of which I partake and which I share with others. They seem to derive their aptitude for being symbols and for being communicative from that antecedent tradition. Thus, such symbols—meant to represent thoughts, feelings, and so forth, in a form that can be perceived by our senses— owe their capacity for representation to a linguistic tradition we carry within us that has already, to a great extent, determined their form and what they stand for.

(1988, pp. 47–48)

As a form of "hypercathexis" according to which one "is simultaneously open to, in tune with, the 'receiving' system," *resonance* describes a relationship in which the psychic apparatuses of two individuals are put into communication with one another by means of the intimacy engendered by the "other reality" marked by the clinical frame and in a way that goes unspoken, because any attempt to represent it accurately could only achieve the most provisional results before becoming too disruptive to be sustained, provoking its disappearance. However, when Loewald suggests in this passage that *writing* is a means by which an individual psychic apparatus can be made to resonate *with itself*, auto-affectively individuating itself by appropriating the tradition of a spectral past that had never been present, he is indicating that something on the order of a "gap"—with everything we have seen this concept implies: temporal space, rhythm, repetition, articulation, *differance*—inhabits the "unfound" essence of the individual psyche. This would be what makes possible not only the individual psyche's singularity but its capacity for further individuation, which would also be the possibility of its therapeutic transformation.

Such writing, of which the voice would be a subset, and which for Loewald is an example of a more generalizable principle, would constitute the "differentiating processes… conceptualized as primary internalizations and externalizations" of the spectral fund of this "most primitive and undifferentiated" experience, always in the background and never having been deposited in the absolute past entirely. The capacity to cultivate and to draw on this intensely personal yet collective fund exists only to the extent that we are capable of appropriating and of contributing to tradition, to what Derrida called the archive, which is both living and dead, both "revolutionary *and* traditional" (Derrida 1995, p. 7; emphasis added). Constantly internalizing and externalizing (reading and writing) and thus weaving together that which constitutes a world, one "of which I partake and which I share with others"—which is to say a world that is irreducibly symbolic and therefore worthy of preservation—I/we generate a space in which to live. This is auto-affection as symbolization as the possibility of history, prior to any metaphysical opposition between subjects and objects. Again we are confronted with a way of thinking symbolization beyond mere cognition, as something that does not belong "to" or "in" the mind but that *operates* at the transitional boundary *between* mind and world—a boundary that symbolization also works to open up and to cause to resonate, allowing mind and world, self and other, to appear *as* themselves and only *in*

The spectrality of the clinical frame   **67**

*relation* to one another. The psychoanalytic clinical frame would be a technology of this spectral, non-metaphysical opening.

## Notes

1  The relationship between mind and thing considered from the perspectives of psycho-analysis and deconstruction is the central topic of Alan Bass's recent *Fetishism, Psychoanalysis and Philosophy: The Iridescent Thing* (2018). In his prior work, to which I am indebted, Bass (2000, 2006) has developed an extensive account of the existential dimension of the classical analytic stance, and has demonstrated that a neutral clinical frame cannot be separated from an interpretive process. It is this particular point that concerns me here.

2  This is not to deny the possibility of telematic articulations of the clinical frame, such as via the telephone or via Skype and other forms of tele-technology today. Such alterations of the classical frame, however, call for extremely meticulous analyses, both theoretical as well as clinical, all of the resources for which psychoanalysis as a discipline does not possess and that would therefore require an interdisciplinary approach. In the next chapter I will show, following Derrida, who follows Freud on this matter, that at the heart of the "living presence" of the patient and analyst in the room together there is already a telematic or tele*graphic* relationship at work.

3  In their Editors' Introduction to the recently published volume, *Reconsidering the Moveable Frame in Psychoanalysis: Its Function and Structure in Psychoanalytic Theory* (2018), Adrienne Harris and Isaac Tylim write that: "The frame is perhaps one of the spots in psycho-analysis where psyche and world come into contact, a place where the psychoanalytic project is both protected and challenged" (p. 1). My argument in this chapter very enthu-siastically echoes this claim, both about the frame as a site of "contact" between mind and world, and about everything that a thinking about the frame does both to protect and to challenge psychoanalysis by calling its most deeply ingrained prejudices about the relationship between mind and world into question (a logic of what both protects and challenges is the topic of my Chapter 4). Unfortunately, Harris and Tylim do not draw out the radical implications of this "spot" where "psyche and world come into con-tact." To do so would require a very broad reorganization of our thinking about psyche and world and about the relationship between them—in other words, a deconstruction of metaphysics. Interestingly, they do see that Derrida's work could be instrumental in thinking about issues that surround the clinical frame, but they only grasp the potential contained in his contributions in a highly limited fashion: "Derrida poses the question of whether computers or machines in general may destroy spontaneity, going so far as to question whether they may render obsolete the existence and necessity of the psyche" (p. 6). It may be true that Derrida occasionally posed questions such as these, but they are far from the most challenging questions his work raises concerning the relationship between psychoanalysis and the machine.

4  An analogy to a phenomenon investigated by developmental psychology might be useful here. In their exhaustive empirical study of infancy, Mahler, Pine and Bergman (1975) established a universal subphase of the process of separation-individuation which they called "practicing." They claim that this occurs from about six months to eighteen months of age. It involves a situation where, in beginning to pursue its autonomy from the care-giver, the infant can be observed crawling away from the caregiver while repetitively looking back towards the caregiver before returning to its position of security in being *held* by the caregiver. "Practicing" is therefore an infant's experimental practice of dif-ferentiating (separating-individuating) itself. For all the apparent difficulties of his mode

**68** The spectrality of the clinical frame

of argument, Derrida is showing us that *thinking* always involves precisely this kind of experimental practice of differentiation and return. As something other than obsessive self-reflection, thought always involves a taking leave of oneself and a returning to oneself predicated on the *risk* of a certain irrecuperable loss: "To risk meaning nothing is to start to play, and first to enter into the play of *differance*" (1981, p. 14).

5 In what follows I will refer to the original English translation of Bleger's essay which appeared in the *International Journal of Psychoanalysis* in 1967. It should be acknowledged that the essay was recently retranslated for a volume in which it was collected together with Bleger's 1967 book *Symbiosis and Ambiguity* (Churcher and Bleger, 2013). Overall, the 2013 translation is unquestionably an improvement upon the earlier translation. However, the more recent translators substitute the word "setting" for the word "frame" in rendering the Spanish *encuadre*. The reason they give for doing so is that in the original text Bleger also uses the Spanish *marco*, which the 1967 translation renders as "bounds" or "limits," for which the 2013 translators prefer "framework," which then must be distinguished from "frame" by "setting" (pp. xli–xlii). "Frame" might have been acceptable for *encuadre* if *marco* could have been rendered as "mark," which would not have been awkward for readers familiar with deconstruction. As the translators themselves acknowledge, with a nod to Saussure (and perhaps implicitly to Derrida), because language is always constituted as a system of differences the work of translation always involves irreducible losses and therefore an openness to new and different editions. I have therefore chosen to retain the original term "frame" to indicate this irreducible openness, and to highlight the fact that the uncontrollably dynamic economy of "verbal nouns" like work, frame, process, mark, limit and binding was something with which Derrida was explicitly and insistently concerned.

6 Freud was very clear in indicating as much when, for example, at the beginning of the 1913 technique paper "On Beginning the Treatment" he likened psychoanalysis to the game of chess where only the opening moves could be subject to any kind of calculation, what follows thereafter being vastly too complex to hope for any kind of formal guideline. This same point was made at the opening of "Recommendations to Physicians on the Psycho-Analytic Method of Treatment" (1912) concerning the meaning of "method" or "technique" from the vantage point of psychoanalysis. Freud's papers on technique are all about strategy in this sense rather than formalism. Nevertheless, Bleger's struggle over the implications of the word "technique" is telling in this context.

7 Although I prefer Joan Stambaugh's superior translation of *Being and Time* (1996), Macquarrie and Robinson's (1962) original translation of these terms as "readiness-to-hand" and "presence-at-hand," while awkward, has the advantage of retaining in both instances Heidegger's reference to the hand, which is crucial and should be kept in mind.

## References

Bass, A. (2000). *Difference and Disavowal: The Trauma of Eros.* Stanford, CA: Stanford University Press.

Bass, A. (2006). *Interpretation and Difference: The Strangeness of Care.* Stanford, CA: Stanford University Press.

Bass, A. (2018). *Fetishism, Psychoanalysis and Philosophy: The Iridescent Thing.* New York: Routledge.

Bion, W.R. (1967). "Notes on memory and desire," *Psychoanalytic Forum*, 2: 271–286.

Bleger, J. (1967) "Psycho-Analysis of the Psycho-Analytic Frame." *International Journal of Psycho-Analysis.* Pp. 511–519.

The spectrality of the clinical frame **69**

Churcher, J., & Bleger, L., Eds. (2013). *Symbiosis and Ambiguity: A Psychoanalytic Study.* New York: Routledge.

Derrida, J. (1973). *Speech and Phenomena.* Trans. D. Allison. Evanston, IL: Northwestern University Press.

Derrida, J. (1976). *Of Grammatology.* Trans. G. Spivak. Baltimore, MD: Johns Hopkins University Press.

Derrida, J. (1978). *Writing and Difference.* Trans. A. Bass. Chicago, IL: University of Chicago Press.

Derrida, J. (1981). *Positions.* Trans. A. Bass. Chicago, IL: University of Chicago Press.

Derrida, J. (1982). "*Différance.*" *Margins—of Philosophy.* Trans. A. Bass. Chicago, IL: University of Chicago Press. Pp. 1–28

Derrida, J. (1987). *The Truth in Painting.* Trans. G. Bennington and I. Mcleod. Chicago, IL: University of Chicago Press.

Derrida, J. (1994). *Specters of Marx: The State of the Debt, The Work of Mourning & the New International.* Trans. P. Kamuf. New York: Routledge.

Derrida, J. (1995). *Archive Fever: A Freudian Impression.* Trans. E. Prenowitz. Chicago, IL: University of Chicago Press.

Faimberg, H. (2012). "José Bleger's Dialectical Thinking." *International Journal of Psycho-Analysis,* 93(4): 981–992.

Freud, S. (1912). "Recommendations to physicians practicing psycho-analysis." S.E. 12.

Freud, S. (1913). "On Beginning the Treatment." S.E. 12.

Harris, A., & Tylim, I., Eds. (2018). *Reconsidering the Moveable Frame in Psychoanalysis: Its Function and Structure in Psychoanalytic Theory.* New York: Routledge.

Heidegger, M. (1962). *Being and Time.* Trans. John Macquarie and Edward Robinson. Cambridge, MA: Blackwell.

Heidegger, M. (1971a). "The Origin of the Work of Art." In: *Poetry, Language, Thought.* Trans. A. Hofstadter. New York: Harper Perennial. Pp. 15–86.

Heidegger, M. (1971b). "The Thing." In: *Poetry, Language, Thought.* Trans. A. Hofstadter. New York: Harper Perennial. Pp. 163–184.

Heidegger, M. (1996). *Being and Time.* Trans. Joan Stambaugh. Albany, NY: SUNY Press.

Loewald, H. (1988). *Sublimation: An Essay in Theoretical Psychoanalysis.* New Haven, CT: Yale University Press.

Mahler, M., Pine, F., & Bergman, A. (1975). *The Psychological Birth of the Human Infant: Symbiosis and Individuation.* New York: Basic Books.

Milner, M. (1987a). "The framed gap." In: *The Suppressed Madness of Sane Men: Forty-Four Years of Exploring Psychoanalysis.* New York: Routledge. Pp. 79–82.

Milner, M. (1987b). "The role of illusion in symbol formation." In: *The Suppressed Madness of Sane Men: Forty-Four Years of Exploring Psychoanalysis.* New York: Routledge. Pp. 83–113.

Winnicott, D.W. (1965). "Communicating and not communicating leading to a study of certain opposites." In: *The Maturational Processes and the Facilitating Environment.* New York: International Universities Press, 1965. Pp. 179–192.

# 3

# A NEW METRICS OF CLINICAL TIME

Building on what we have so far encountered about the nature of transformative dialogue and about the framework that makes such dialogue—which can be considered, from a perspective informed by deconstruction, something both prior to and in excess of an intersubjective, dialectical exchange—possible as a therapeutic, clinical practice, this chapter assembles a series of reflections on Heidegger's expanded notion of *thinking*, on Derrida's expanded notion of *writing*, and on what it means to speak of psychoanalytic *technique*.

In the first section I sketch out Heidegger's reflections in his essay, "The end of philosophy and the task of thinking" (2002), relating these backwards to themes developed in *Being and Time* (1996) and *Kant and the Problem of Metaphysics* (1990), as well as forward to Derrida's development of an expanded notion of writing in the three volumes that announced him as a major thinker in 1967 (I will limit my focus to *Of Grammatology* [1976]). In the second section, I explore themes in Derrida's later work—specifically, the essay "Telepathy" (2007)—that explicitly address the relationship between deconstruction and psychoanalysis, and that concern Freud's comments about unconscious communication and his comparison of the analytic relationship with the mechanism of the telephone. In the final section, in an effort to deepen an appreciation of the relationship between thinking, writing, and clinical practice, I offer a close reading of a series of important essays by the contemporary British Kleinian analyst Dana Birksted-Breen, whose work is among the most interesting projects—one of several, though it would take many more readings to demonstrate this—where the contemporary psychoanalytic literature appears to be heading in a direction already anticipated by deconstruction, without yet recognizing that this is the case.

**72** A new metrics of clinical time

## The end of philosophy and the task of writing

At the opening of his essay, "The end of philosophy and the task of thinking," Heidegger remarks, "The title designates the attempt at a reflection which persists in questioning. The questions are paths to an answer. If the answer could be given, the answer would consist in a transformation of thinking, not in a propositional statement about a matter at stake" (2002, p. 55). In this way Heidegger announces that what follows will not constitute a manifesto. No simple answer will be given that could instruct us on what the coming task for thought is. The answer will instead involve a transformation of the one who asks. There is no way to determine in what this transformation will "consist," only that it will "persist" in questioning. Since transformation is not an event that can be given immediately, what follows will be an open-ended attempt not at answering the question but at working through what it means that we are able to pose the question in the first place. Heidegger thus intimates that the task of thinking will require an effort at abandoning the framework that opposes questions and answers. This will be in order to open "paths" that facilitate enduring transformation and change. The task of thinking will be to cultivate the openness of pathways for transformation over time. This effort cannot be settled by the end of our reading of the essay; its success will be determined by its lingering persistence later on.

Characteristically, Heidegger identifies philosophy with metaphysics. The intrinsic link between metaphysics and representational thinking is the generalization of the Aristotelian concept of time as a linear, progressive series of now-points. "Metaphysics," Heidegger writes, "thinks being in the manner of representational thinking which gives reasons" (p. 56). To give reasons is to describe causes that by definition precede effects, and that explain (as a way of appearing to control) those effects by governing them from a distance. This distance authorizes itself with reference to the concept of origin. A cause is the origin of an effect, and in such a way that establishes an irrefutable hierarchy. Both causes and effects appear as past and present now-points that communicate with one another: A cause is a "now" that produces an effect as another "now" that is subsequent and therefore subordinate. These paths of communication between past causes and present effects, when they appear transparent, form explanations. To give a reason for something is to trace its origin to a past cause possessed of the ability to govern and thereby to explain. Heidegger calls this kind of thinking "representational" because it thinks causes and effects together as forms of presence, that is, ontically as objects (beings). This is why metaphysics, as Heidegger indicates, can ever only think being as cause, origin, or ground: "What characterizes metaphysical thinking which grounds the ground for beings is the fact that metaphysical thinking departs from what is present in its presence, and thus represents it in terms of its ground as something grounded" (p. 56). As cause, origin, or ground, being can only appear as something "in" time, and in such a way that time is thereby rendered as something spatial and so remains thought only metaphysically.

Lest we interpret the title of the essay to mean that philosophy has come to an end in the sense either of its completion or its exhaustion, Heidegger warns us that this would be "premature" (p. 57). To the extent that philosophy in the form of modern technological science both realizes the essence of metaphysical thinking and appears to do away with the need for philosophy entirely, this end must not be thought in the form of closure. Where metaphysics has reached its end it has both effaced itself and proliferated its manner of thinking to every corner of the globe. Both everywhere and nowhere at once in the era of global technology, the metaphysical conception of being as presence has become so transparently self-evident that it no longer appears in need of being asked after. According to Heidegger, this ever-evolving failure of metaphysical thinking to reflect on its own origins and assumptions gives rise to the modern scientific attitude. This attitude is one in which, "The operational and model character of representational-calculative thinking becomes dominant" (pp. 58–59).

Why is Heidegger talking about science in this context? Modern technological science would have us believe that thinking scientifically as a form of representation-calculation indicates the end of thinking metaphysically as a form of speculation or mere belief. Modern science claims to have emerged from the end of metaphysics, as the superseding of a religious paradigm. Heidegger's point, here as elsewhere, is that this is not at all the case: the techno-scientific manipulation of the environment, made possible by the ideological framework that thinks fundamentally in terms of an absolute opposition between subjects and objects, does not dispel the illusions of metaphysics or of religion (which Heidegger gathers together under the heading "onto-theology"); to the contrary, it expresses the essence of this way of thinking and operationalizes it globally, destroying anything that gets in its path. The subject/object opposition of modern science translates into a secular register the transcendental opposition between the earthly and the heavenly realms, itself an elaboration of the Platonic opposition of the material and the ideal. The onto-theological forgetting of the question of being, which for centuries was elaborated as the identification of being with God in religious monotheism, today assumes the form of the deification of the human in its capacity to exercise dominion over its environment technologically. Hence the "end" of metaphysics is not the exhaustion but the complete realization of metaphysics as contemporary techno-science, in which representational-calculative thinking becomes dominant. Heidegger identifies this dominance with the rise of the then emergent science of cybernetics, the basis for the contemporary cognitive science industry.

At this point Heidegger takes up the second part of his title by asking, "*What task is reserved for thinking at the end of philosophy?*" He immediately offers an answer in the form of another (though altogether different kind of) question: "The mere thought of such a task of thinking must sound strange to us. A thinking which can be neither metaphysics nor science?" (p. 59; emphasis in original). The first of these two questions implies the possibility of an answer; the second draws attention to the fact that no answer would seem to make sense, at least not where representational-calculative thinking has become dominant. "Neither metaphysics nor science"

**74** A new metrics of clinical time

plays on the fact that Heidegger is at work dismantling the familiar opposition between these two terms. The effort to think beyond this opposition cannot rely on the introduction of a third term but must prepare a transformative reorganization of our ordinary way of thinking. Again, this reorganization will not have been achieved by the end of the essay, but Heidegger will spend the rest of the text preparing the way for such a possibility as that which cannot be calculated in advance if it is to be more than an empty repetition of familiar problematics: "Thinking must first learn what remains reserved and in store for thinking to get involved in. It prepares for its own transformation in this learning" (p. 60).

In a series of pages that swiftly gather together some of the greatest names in the philosophical tradition—Descartes, Kant, Hegel, Nietzsche, Husserl—tracing their projects each back to Plato in terms of the valorization of understanding by analogy to the "light" of Reason, Heidegger argues that what remains unthought in the history of the Western tradition is the "opening" that would first allow the light of Reason to shine, that would allow for the (more than metaphorical) opposition of light and darkness, and that would be neither light nor darkness (neither knowledge nor ignorance, neither active nor passive, presence nor absence) but which would perceive in advance how these oppositions come forth and generate effects in the form of the historical tradition. This opening would be the *possibility* of Reason (as shared, universal), which cannot be thought according to the dictates of Reason, logic, or representation-calculation as an origin in the ordinary, causal sense.

Heidegger also designates this non-original origin of rational, causal thought "clearing" (p. 65) by analogy to cutting a path through a forest. At issue in the task of thinking, for Heidegger, is thinking the possibility of thinking as what conditions the emergence of Reason as the origin of the Western tradition. Philosophy is the valorization of Reason as the essence of thought that gives rise to the tradition of science. Today, cognitive science expresses this effort at valorization by dispensing with history and with the history of its own development in the achievement of the metaphysical framework that opposes the subjective and the objective rendered as obvious, uncircumventible ground. Cognitive science presents itself as the most effective means of manipulating the opposition of the subjective and the objective by naturalizing this opposition in such a way that makes any effort to call it into question seem counterintuitive and obscure. Cognitive science derives its power from the metaphysical framework that refuses any effort to deny that we are only subjects that are capable of relating only to objects to which we are absolutely, constitutively opposed.

It is this concealed movement of naturalization for which Heidegger attempts to provide a history and to move into crisis. The task of thinking today is to think the history of this opposition *as* history and not as eternal, metaphysical truth. Since Descartes and Kant, the concepts of the subjective and the objective have encouraged the identification of the advance of science with the advance of technology as a merely artificial tool for manipulating the natural environment. Whereas Derrida will deconstruct the opposition between the natural and the artificial, leading him to embrace what is original yet historical in the cognitive-cybernetic project, Heidegger will continue to insist that metaphysics first emerges from a historical effort at opposing self and environment that gives rise to imperative frameworks of administration, technocracy, and control.

The opening chapter of Derrida's *Of Grammatology*—"The end of the book and the beginning of writing"—is an effort at resituating everything that Heidegger had announced in "The end of philosophy and the task of thinking." Derrida radicalizes Heidegger's expanded notion of *thinking*—as both active and passive, conjoining history as past and history as openness to future possibility—as *writing*. This expanded notion of writing rethinks thinking on a materialist basis, or in excess of the opposition of the material and the ideal, in order to think the relationship between the human and its environment in terms of the transformative effects of material inscription. The chapter is an updated and critically transformed version of Heidegger's essay that thinks being altogether differently by refusing to oppose human being to the essence of technology: "…a certain sort of question about the meaning and origin of writing precedes, or at least merges with, a certain type of question about the meaning and origin of technics" (Derrida 1976, p. 8). In the history of the reception of Derrida's work, particularly as it has been determined by literary theory and cultural studies, this statement has been overshadowed by the overworked and rather less challenging, "*il n'y a pas de hors-texte*" (p. 158). But it is this claim concerning "the meaning and origin of technics" that provides, if such a gesture is possible, the position statement of the *Grammatology*.

For Derrida, Heidegger's thinking about the reciprocal openness of self and world remains too metaphysical in its valorization of being as a term that oversees the task of thinking and that thereby inadvertently returns us to a representational approach. The beginning of writing, in Derrida's sense, is what Heidegger calls opening as the essence or origin of language rendered architecturally as the "house of being" (Heidegger 1993). In so designating this essence or origin, however, Derrida indicates the inadequacy of conceiving essence or origin in metaphysical terms as an original presence that governs causally. This is the point at which Derrida uses the resources of Heidegger's own thinking against itself: whereas for Heidegger being is a privileged term for conceiving the openness of Da-sein as immanent, worldly structure, Derrida's writing inscribes this processive structure without a governing term within a conceptual economy that traces the movement of becoming-other that Heidegger insists *is* thinking (i.e. the transformation of the one who asks in the act of authentic questioning) at the end of philosophy or as neither metaphysics nor science.

As so often still needs to be made clear to most readers, *Of Grammatology* is not an attempt to outline a science of writing. Derrida's effort is rather to demonstrate how such a science is strictly impossible without calling into question the very framework of the modern scientific project by forcing a reconsideration of the relationship between the human and the technical, beyond the valorization of the voice *qua* consciousness as the articulation of the "living present." Beyond the living present as a circuit of reduction that generates self-presence in the event of hearing-oneself-speak,

## 76 A new metrics of clinical time

Derrida locates a machinic operation of the *grammē* that indicates a kind of thought appearing not in the form of the *phonē* (sound or voice) but as writing: what Derrida calls "arche-writing" (p. 56) as a non-subjective writing that writes itself, a kind of thinking that the ungovernable play of general material inscription *is*.

Like Lacan, Derrida pushes Heidegger's claim that "language speaks" (2013, p. 188) towards an appreciation of the autonomy of the signifier. More radically than Lacan, Derrida sees that this autonomy overturns the privilege of the voice and inaugurates a new way of thinking about writing as originary technicity. This is what Derrida elaborates as a logic of the supplement: "'Signifier of the signifier' describes ... the movement of language: in its origin, to be sure, but one can already suspect that an origin whose structure can be expressed as 'signifier of the signifier' conceals and erases itself in its own production" (1976, p. 7). He identifies this generative erasure as an effacement that overwhelms the limits of language and that deregulates the production of signs: "this overwhelming and this effacement have the same meaning" (ibid.). Rather than, as for Heidegger and Lacan, providing access to the truth of discourse around which language circulates (either universally as "being," or as the "primordial signifier" that fixes a particular subject's identity), Derrida argues that the origin or essence of thought to which language refers is perpetually deferred and cannot be made present. "Essence" or "origin" thus becomes technical "supplement," designating what secondarily befalls, but in such a way as to constitute, the experience of the living present. This is why Derrida is kinder to the import of cybernetics than Heidegger is in his attempt to determine what thinking must become at the end of philosophy as metaphysics, and why he sees in cognitive science a powerful sign that it is eminently capable of deconstructing itself.

According to Heidegger, "Perhaps there is a thinking which is more sober than the irresistible race of rationalization and the sweeping character of cybernetics. Presumably it is precisely this sweeping quality which is extremely irrational" (2002, p. 72). In this appeal to Reason to resist the irrationality of rationalization, Heidegger returns us to the very tradition that he wishes to destabilize and that makes the "sweeping quality" of contemporary techno-science "irresistible." This is the authoritarian element in Heidegger's discourse that Derrida intends to eliminate while refining the effort at deconstructing the metaphysical basis of the modern scientific project. For Derrida, what is required to encourage thought today in the era of representation-calculation is not a more sober form of poetic reflection, but a more rigorous spirit of critical, playful production:

> If the theory of cybernetics is by itself to oust all metaphysical concepts—including the concepts of soul, of life, of value, of choice, of memory—which until recently served to separate the machine from man, it must conserve the notion of writing, trace, grammè, or grapheme until its own historico-metaphysical character is also exposed.
>
> (1976, p. 9)

Derrida here grasps what is exciting and revelatory about the machine metaphor, without succumbing uncritically to the pull towards positivistic or concrete thinking that such an excitement typically involves. Where the machine is taken to reveal the truth of the operations of the psyche, this necessitates a rethinking of the value and authority classically attributed to the concept of truth conceived as the correct representation of an object by a subject. If the modern scientific project is to break rigorously with the humanist refusal to entertain any comparison between the human and the machine, or between life and program, it must proceed via a thematics of writing as what can be demonstrated to resist all forms of metaphysical enclosure and control. This necessity informs the essential lesson of the *Grammatology*: to respond to and to resist control is to write.

As a materialist rather than an idealist practice—or rather, as a practice that uproots the founding philosophical gesture that opposes the material and the ideal, exposing what he will later call spectrality—Derrida's expanded notion of *writing* reconfigures Heidegger's similarly expanded notion of *thinking*. As a practice performed in the presence of an other who is not present, yet whose absence marks the non-sensuous materiality of a form of presence that cannot be opposed to absence as in a classical, decidable logic, writing resists oppositional thinking and refuses practices of exclusion that continue to inform Heidegger's valorization of being (as well as, certainly, the horror of his politics). This resistance appears at the end of Derrida's essay "Differance" (1982b) where, in relation to Heidegger on "The Anaximander Fragment," Derrida refuses "the alliance of speech and Being in the unique word, in the finally proper name" (p. 27). This is why, whereas Heideggerian thinking gathers, Derridean writing disseminates.

Furthermore, where voice and writing are no longer conceived of as opposed to one another, what is foregrounded is the irreducibly *technical* dimension of all forms of articulation or of articulated difference—linguistic, biological, relational, temporal and otherwise—such that these disparate domains can be assembled together under the heading of a general "grammatology." The object of such a science, however, would not be an objectively present object in a classical sense, requiring us to think differently about the limits of science itself. This would not be simply to oppose science, because it is the valorization of that very gesture for which a critical account is being provided, but an effort to establish a form of thinking that is "neither metaphysics nor science." Heidegger's non-original "opening" is in this way inscribed as a form of technical articulation in the distinctly ambiguous Derridean term *brisure* as "hinge" and/or "break" (1976, p. 65), as that which both conjoins and separates according to an undecidable, non-classical logic. This logic will not necessarily explain anything, but it will produce effects of coordination and articulation that challenge the values traditionally assigned to presence and absence, and to everything this irreducibly metaphysical opposition governs.

It is for this reason, and in conjunction with his comments on cybernetics as a necessary passage which the deconstruction of metaphysics must traverse, that psychoanalysis appears to Derrida as a discourse in many ways already more sophisticated and more scientifically advanced than cognitive science. It is in the

**78** A new metrics of clinical time

Freudian concept of the psychical *apparatus* that Derrida discovers a powerful resource for deconstructing all attempts "to separate the machine from man." This discovery potentially situates psychoanalysis beyond metaphysics, as an experimental form of relationality that cannot be figured by classical oppositions such as those between subjects and objects, past and present, matter and spirit, mind and world.

## A terrifying telephone

In an interview in which he spoke of photography as viewed through the lens of deconstruction, Derrida stated:

> In a tradition that belongs both to common language and to philosophy, "passivity" is opposed to "activity." But the Kantian-Heideggerian (also no doubt Husserlian) analysis to which I referred a moment ago concerns temporality as a pure auto-affective synthesis in which activity is itself passivity. This problematic is indispensable, even if it may be unfamiliar in the milieus in which a competent discourse on photography is practiced. The meditations are numerous; certainly, they are difficult and nuanced, but the link with the specificity of photography is perhaps best indicated, although indirectly, in the fact that this meditation on auto-affection as temporality passes through the *schematism* of the transcendental *imagination*. It is a question of the image, of the production of the fantastic, of an imagination that is productive in the very constitution of time and in originary temporality.
>
> (2010, pp. 13–14; emphases in original)

The milieus in which this topic remains unfamiliar include psychoanalysis—another discipline concerned with the production of the fantastic. The question of originary temporality is the question of memory, non-metaphysically conceived. What is memory if it is not only a passive receptacle that merely registers information, but that simultaneously and actively repeats and refers, and in such a way that these two (active and passive) functions determine one another, each as the condition of the other's possibility? This is memory as "pure auto-affective synthesis." Auto-affective again means ecstatically related to itself as open rather than substantively closed in upon itself. In *Being and Time* Heidegger had formulated auto-affection in terms of time-temporalizing-itself as the structure of Da-sein as ecstatic openness: Da-sein actively-passively *is* toward its future, stretching along as a "lingering" (1996, p. 113) that links birth to death, in such a way that makes human experience meaningful as the site of a destining that is both individual and collective. Time-temporalizing-itself is what Da-sein must be in order for there to be a meaningful relation to beings in general; in the absence of this ecstatic openness there are only objects confronting one another meaninglessly in the mode of objective presence (*Vorhandenheit*). Auto-affection describes a form of self-relation that must insist prior to any relation to objects, whether external or internal. It is because Da-sein exists as open, self-othering process that things can be related to at all. Ecstatic time as auto-affective, open self-relation is the possibility of "world."

A new metrics of clinical time **79**

For Kant, the transcendental subject is atemporal because space and time are *a priori* categories that the mind brings to experience in order to constitute the horizon of experience as such. Heidegger's basic yet profound insight is that this complicates what it means to speak of space and time as *a priori* categories. Such categories cannot be temporally prior or spatially outside—they cannot be "before" our experience of the world as what we bring "to" the world in the ordinary temporal sense of "before" and the ordinary spatial sense of "to" that we receive from our having brought space and time to our experience as categories that organize our experience *as* experience. We cannot use the terms provided by the categories that organize our experience to explain those categories themselves, just as we cannot use consciousness as a model for thinking about unconscious processes. Time as Kantian *a priori* fundamental category must therefore be more temporal than time as we normally think of it—it cannot be thought spatially (geometrically) as a linear succession of now-points. Furthermore, Heidegger argues, if time for Kant is the pure internal sense, this more originally temporal time—time-temporalizing-itself—is what we *are*.

In *Kant and the Problem of Metaphysics*, Heidegger writes, "time as pure self-affection is not found 'in the mind' 'along with' pure apperception. Rather, as the ground for the possibility of selfhood, time already lies within pure apperception, and so it first makes the mind into mind" (1990, p. 134). What makes the mind into mind (i.e. internal subjectivity) is the retreat from the openness of Da-sein as being-in-the-world. What triggers this retreat is anxiety and uncanniness attendant upon "thrownness" (1996, p. 127ff.) as the encounter with Da-sein's essential finitude. What makes mind into mind is thus an encounter with the other that ultimately cannot be figured metaphysically as a relation between a subject and an object, but that must be converted into such a relation by closing itself off in order to forget being *as* being. For Heidegger, this is what Kant demonstrates in prioritizing the transcendental subject over and against the transcendental imagination between the A and B editions of the *Critique of Pure Reason*. This inaugural gesture ushers in the era of modern technological science and the kind of representational-calculative fact-mindedness it engenders.

In his enigmatic essay "Telepathy," Derrida (2007) integrates his previous thinking about the transcendental imagination, time, technics, and psychoanalysis. He addresses Freud's conflicted preoccupation with the possibility of non-sensuous communicative processes. The clinical investigations of psychoanalysis had led Freud to conceive of a paradoxical proximity-in-distance that authorizes a thinking about the clinic as a scene in which the unconscious of the patient telepathically "transmits" itself to the unconscious of the analyst, whose task it is to reconstruct the content of these transmissions. In "Recommendations to physicians practicing psycho-analysis" (1912), Freud writes:

> To put it in a formula: [the analyst] must turn his own unconscious like a receptive organ towards the transmitting unconscious of the patient. He must adjust himself to the patient as a telephone receiver is adjusted to the

**80** A new metrics of clinical time

transmitting microphone. Just as the receiver converts back into sound waves the electric oscillations in the telephone line which were set up by sound waves, so the doctor's unconscious is able, from the derivatives of the unconscious which are transmitted to him, to reconstruct that unconscious, which has determined the patient's free-associations.

(pp. 115–116)

Reconvening everything he had written about the technological metaphor of the psychic apparatus as a writing machine from "Freud and the Scene of Writing" on, Derrida, implicitly commenting on this passage, writes:

the telepathic process would be physical in itself, except at its two extremes; one extreme is reconverted (*sich wieder umsetz*) into the psychical same at the other extreme. Therefore, the "analogy" with other "transpositions," other "conversions" (*Umsetzungen*), would be indisputable: for example, the analogy of "speaking and listening on the telephone." Between rhetoric and the psychophysical relation, within each one and from one to the other, there is only translation (*Ubersetzung*), metaphor (*Ubertragung*), "transfers," "transpositions," analogical conversions, and above all transfers of transfers: *uber, meta, tele* … And the telematic *tekhne* is not a paradigm or materialized example of another thing, *it is that* (compare our mystic writing pad, it is an analogous problematic, it all communicates by telephone). But once again, a terrifying telephone … this physical equivalent of the psychic act.

(2007, p. 242; emphases in original)

In referring to "a terrifying telephone," Derrida is putting together Freud's intuition as to the telepathic nature of the analytic situation with Heidegger's thinking about anxiety, uncanniness, and ecstatic time. His point is that if we read Heidegger's account of the anxiety-provoking nature of the disclosure of being *as* being, in which Da-sein encounters its finitude as openness to world as being-in and as being-together-with beyond the subject/object divide, alongside Freud's intuitions about telepathic, non-sensuous material structures at work in the clinical relationship, we can begin to understand Freud's reluctance to engage more systematically with this topic as having to do with more than his concern for an appearance of scientific respectability. Unconscious communication is the mark of time as ecstatic openness; it reveals a "hetero-affective" (Derrida 1998, p. 28) dimension of auto-affection that redoubles anxiety and that demonstrates that the clinical encounter between patient and analyst can function as an existential disclosure of being *as* being—an effort at what *Being and Time* had called "the most radical *individuation.*" The "terrifying telephone" that is the "physical equivalent of the psychic act" is the analytic situation itself and all properties that bear on the construction and maintenance of the clinical frame.

Generalizing this insight to cover the entirety of the clinical field, Derrida writes, "there is only tele-analysis, they will have to draw all the conclusions as we do, get their concept of the 'analytic situation' to swallow a new metrics of time" (2007, p. 232). The "they" at issue is presumably the analytic community, the "we" the community bound by the effort to deconstruct metaphysics, brought together by a rethinking of the analytic situation—and as a situation that is not just specific to psychoanalysis but to deconstruction itself, as an effort to rethink the relational beyond the horizon of the intersubjective—as the elaboration of a "new metrics of time." Putting aside for a moment Derrida's prescient choice of analogy in anticipating this labor (why "swallow" [*faire avaler*]?—we will come back to this), we can say that this is the moment in the entirety of Derrida's work that gives us a sense of what integrating deconstruction with psychoanalysis as a clinical practice and not just as a theory would consist in. It would concern above all an effort to rethink the nature of analytic neutrality as both receptive and constructive, and its relation to free association as both spontaneous and passive, as both auto-affective (active-passive) and hetero-affective (individuating-relational) processes that would push for a "new metrics of time" conceived as the analytic situation itself in its irreducibly *technical* dimension.

Rest assured, none of this is quite as complicated as may initially seem. What Derrida is describing—what was always at issue in his work, beginning with the introduction of the expanded notion of writing—is an experience that clinicians are in a uniquely privileged position to appreciate. Taking up the very same passage from Freud's "Recommendations to physicians" that so intrigues Derrida, Christopher Bollas writes:

> The Freudian Pair constitutes a mixed sequential temporality. Although the session is part of some more local interest and binds many prior interests into a shared space for a while, it is also a temporal collage, as lines of thought pursued in many different temporal rhythms are present at the same time. The psychoanalyst's open-mindedness allows the psychoanalyst to be under the influence of any wave of thought, whatever its frequency. Indeed, the analyst may unconsciously perceive a line of thought which arises momentarily, but whose history long precedes the analysis, removing it from any possibility of translation into consciousness.
>
> Does the psychoanalyst possess a temporal capacity that can operate in varying wavelengths? The repetition of clusters of association, occurring in different temporalities, instructs the analyst's unconscious as to the wavelength of the 'network'.
>
> (2002, pp. 56–57)

Bollas indicates here that the "temporal collage" that constitutes unconscious communication exists "outside"—yet only together *with*—the time of conscious, causal connection. Although consciousness can only discover this secondarily (in Derridean terms: supplementarily), it reveals an originary temporality that cannot be thought in terms of conscious, logical, causal relations. With the very same economy of provisional metaphors that we have been tracking across the

## 82 A new metrics of clinical time

psychoanalytic literature—wavelengths, networks, repetition, rhythms, time and space—Bollas describes what insistently disrupts the conscious time of logical, causal connection while never appearing outside that temporal horizon in which the past or future can only ever appear to have come before or after the present. These disruptions produce effects that indicate this other temporality to be consistently operating even when it is not being attended to. We are always engaged to some extent in this kind of this "telepathic" relation with others, though this is covered over and dissimulated at the level of everyday affairs. The tradition of metaphysics calls this "memory" conceived as a form of subjective retentional storage. A successful analytic treatment gradually brings out into the open and integrates this temporal capacity. This is the meaning of symbolization as a distinctly psychoanalytic concept.

The experience of an analysis is replete with instances in which meaning appears both created and disclosed, in which the impact of past events seems to be finally coming to light, or in which newly coordinated series of past events seem to have been leading up to the present moment. This is even more so the case for the analyst than for the patient:

> There is, then, no single chain of thought: rather… multiple lines of psychic interest, moving through moments of life like some silent radiant intelligence. As the analyst assumes the position of evenly suspended attentiveness, he or she comes under the influence of the unconscious order. Guided by the logic of the patient's chain of ideas, the analyst at some point will *retrospectively discover* what the patient has, in part at least, been talking about.
>
> (Bollas 2002, p. 17; emphasis added)

The analytic stance of neutral receptivity—what Bollas calls "the psychoanalyst's open-mindedness"—as neither stably, decidably active or passive, describes temporality (memory) as pure auto-affective synthesis. What this means is that, where the past appears to come "after" the present (via clinical "retrospective discovery," prior to which it might seem as if nothing significant is occurring), this is passivity as activity. In those uncanny moments where the future seems have preceded, come "before" the present (as in the experience of *moira* or fate central to the ancient Greeks—one need only think here of the climax of *Oedipus Rex*), this is activity as passivity. Together these constitute the "temporal collage" of being-together-with as intrinsic to our being-in-the-world which the analytic frame instances. The technique of analytic neutrality foregrounds this relational capacity beyond the metaphysical framework of the intersubjective, and beyond a conception of knowledge as positivist certainty.

Abandoning neutrality and attempting to decide in advance what the patient is talking about—in Heidegger's terms, to "*leap in*" for the other in order to "take his 'care' away from him" (1996, p. 114; emphasis in original)—is a defensive response that shuts down this ecstatic, existential time in which thinking as *anticipatory* openness is able *retrospectively* to discover the existence of unconscious, non-causal "transmissions." As a result of this defensive response, clinical practice becomes an

A new metrics of clinical time **83**

effort at asserting academic theory, and the analyst implicitly assumes the anxiety-relieving stance of the knowledgeable authority figure, which is what the patient, in his own tendency toward closure as a self-present, conscious subject, may implicitly be hoping for or even provoking, if unconsciously. Analysis thereby becomes a pedagogical effort at correcting the patient's distortions and forcing him to accept the analyst's version of reality. This version of reality, like that involved in any effort to enforce authority and to reduce the other to a figure of the same, and regardless of its particular content, invariably issues from a reactive need to forget originary temporality and to insist on the time of consciousness as self-presence. Although he does not have this vocabulary at his disposal, it is precisely this arrangement that Bollas describes as a betrayal of the Freudian spirit:

> If one practices from the Freudian perspective, then one assumes that it will not be possible to follow the material in the here and now on a conscious level: indeed, attempting to do so refuses the very nature of unconscious communication itself. It is an indication of how far some psychoanalysts have drifted from the original paradigm of psychoanalysis that too many analysts require of themselves, their colleagues and their students the 'ability' to follow the patient's meaning in the here and now.
>
> (2002, pp. 77–78, fn.4)

A properly Freudian practice, on this account, cannot be one focused on the here-and-now of conscious time; it must ground itself in unconscious, non-causal temporality via evenly suspended attention and receptive neutral reverie. Not deciding on what the patient "really means," not instructing new generations of analysts on what to listen for in order to fit clinical material into preconceived theoretical categories, and not defensively retreating into a position of conscious knowledge as a source of authority for enforcing universal notions of what would constitute mental health—this is what it would mean to practice psychoanalysis deconstructively.[1]

## A malignantly denuded present

In a series of important essays, Dana Birksted-Breen (2003, 2009, 2012) develops an account of the experience of time specific to the psychoanalytic clinic. With her own take on what is becoming a familiar vocabulary, she outlines what she calls "reverberation time" as this is intrinsic to the uniquely dynamic "tempo" of analytic work. She draws together and integrates complex lines of thought about analytic listening, reverie, the mother–infant matrix, and the unusual experience of temporality intrinsic to the clinical relationship. Like Bollas, she is critical towards those technical approaches predominant in the British and American schools that focus insistently on the here-and-now of the intersubjective interaction:

> I speak of "here and now" technique in a wide sense to cover a way of working that is characterized by frequent interventions aimed at describing

**84** A new metrics of clinical time

> the patient's experience and feelings towards the analyst throughout the
> session. It is a particular way of conceiving of the 'transference interpretation.'
>
> (2012, p. 820)

This "particular way of conceiving of the 'transference interpretation'" insists on transference as distortion—as the subjective distortion of objective truth—and correspondingly it conceives of interpretation as an effort to correct that distortion from a position of authority and knowledge. Against this authoritarian tendency, Birksted-Breen returns us to the practice of evenly suspended attention or reverie as a practice that demands a more complex appreciation of the "tempo" of analytic work:

> The increasingly popular 'here and now' technique lends itself to this pitfall
> [that of 'concrete thinking'] if it is not grounded firmly in a theoretical and
> technical approach resting on the form of temporality described by Freud as
> 'evenly suspended attention' ... sometimes also referred to in the literature as
> 'evenly hovering attention' or 'free-floating attention'. Its main characteristic
> is an unfocused state of mind. Such a state of mind implies a withholding of
> immediate response and thus a duration. In that important way it necessarily
> involves temporality.
>
> (2012, pp. 819–820)

Unlike most ordinary interactions, psychoanalysis opens up a different experience of time—one that both facilitates psychic integration and that allows the transferential relationship to appear exceedingly meaningful. This temporality elaborates itself in the context of the analyst's practice of neutral reverie, as the complement to the patient's efforts at free association. Slowing down the accelerated pace of contemporary life, analytic time allows for the "reverberation" of symbolically articulated experiences in such a way that provides language with a therapeutic capacity, making possible a talking cure that has nothing to do with suggestion, instruction, or coercion. Birksted-Breen writes:

> The transformation we seek in psychoanalysis is double: a transformation
> into language and a transformation into using language in a way that supports
> symbolic thinking. Symbolic thinking underpins psychoanalysis, and yet we
> are confronted repeatedly with how fragile such thinking can be and how
> easily concrete thinking takes over in ways that are not always immediately
> evident when it is the analyst who becomes prey to it. Impasse may always
> have a form of concrete thinking on the part of the analyst, as well as of the
> patient, as its foundation.
>
> (2012, p. 819)

The "double transformation" both of the relation to language and of the way in which language is deployed depends upon an ability to experience time

A new metrics of clinical time **85**

dynamically—to transition fluidly between past and present, memory and perception: "Thinking is what detaches one from the immediate reality into symbolization and brings the possibility of *moving backwards and forward in time*" (2009, p. 39; emphasis in original). *Thinking* here means not being captivated by the *now* of "immediate reality," but "detaching" as facilitating movement in time or *of* time as an ongoing, temporalizing process.

Although Birksted-Breen writes only of the coordination of past and present, memory and perception, we should add a third dimension: future anticipation. The patient not only transitions back and forth between memories of her past and perceptions of her present, she projects forward toward anticipations of her future. Moving backwards and forwards in time does not stop at the present but projects toward the future. In this way desire is generated, the interpretation of which drives the clinical relationship via the handling of the transference. As Birksted-Breen indicates, the cultivation of such a capacity depends upon the repetitively structured space and time of the analytic frame:

> The characteristics of the setting with its strict boundaries in time and space demarcate a particular temporality inside the boundaries, not so much atemporality or timelessness it seems to me as a *bi-temporality*. A specific temporality is given by the analytic pair who will speak of past or present. But whether the analyst chooses to interpret now *or* then, the time within the analytic setting is always now *and* then. The essence of psychoanalysis lies in that double register.
>
> (2009, p. 43; emphases in original)

The "double register" of the "double transformation" that an analysis consists in involves the opening up of what Birksted-Breen elsewhere calls "temporal space" (2012, p. 827). As we have seen in previous chapters, a thinking in terms of temporal space (Derridean diff*e*rance) as the prerequisite condition for symbol formation—in which ideas and experiences are both connected and remain distinct, and in the absence of which concrete thinking and symbolic equation predominate—inevitably emerges when symbolization can no longer be considered an innate and reliable cognitive process but as a capacity that only emerges through practices of repetition, individuation and differentiation. These were practices that Derrida had grouped together under an expanded notion of writing, as that which is capable of generating difference.

The heart of this temporalizing process that both separates (spaces) and connects (binds) ideas in the mind consists in practices of repetition that the analytic setting formalizes—again: coming to the same place, at the same time, day after day. By situating repetition at the heart of the "specific temporality" of clinical experience, Birksted-Breen indicates the link between the open-endedness of an analytic approach and the therapeutic action of the talking cure: the effort to create the temporal space necessary for symbolization. This is not a matter of merely putting things into words, or of speaking what has so far gone unspoken. As we saw

**86** A new metrics of clinical time

in Chapter 2, creating temporal space involves *spacing time* by means of the "strict boundaries" that *inscribe* so as to constitute the analytic frame. What this means is that the clinical contract that both patient and analyst agree to and that keep them each *coming back* to the same place at the same times no matter what the impulse to do otherwise is an essential part of what it means to be able to practice interpretation as a form of therapeutic technique. The stably repetitive nature of the frame in this sense constitutes a calendrical function: a pre-linguistic, non-interpersonal background that structures space and time dynamically, and in such a way that allows the specific temporality of the clinic to be opened up and to function therapeutically by facilitating symbolization.

Norbert Freedman elaborated this same concept of temporal space, which he also called "symbolizing space," as a way of accounting for how language can function mutatively as a vehicle of transformation rather than as a merely technical means of communication (Freedman 1998; Freedman and Lavender 2002; Freedman and Russell 2003). To conceive of language as a tool one simply uses to communicate meaning is to split apart language and time—to think of these as things we have, rather than as integrated dimensions of experience that give rise to the sense of subjectivity or self to begin with. For Freedman, the inability to think symbolically is not a developmental or structural deficiency, but the defensive repudiation of the vulnerability or openness intrinsic to unpredictable, symbolizing processes. Desymbolization, in Freedman's vocabulary, describes active efforts to suppress the establishment of symbolizing connections as a result of the anxiety attendant upon moments of structural integration that express genuine insight and that register difference.

Provocatively, Birksted-Breen locates this same failure of symbolic thinking in those approaches predominant in the British and American schools that focus insistently on the here-and-now of the interpersonal interaction. In this approach, the analyst's frequent interventions concerning the immediate reality of the relational dialogue can make both participants feel that important work is being done, that each is properly doing his or her job, and that no time is being wasted. But this is complicit with efforts to enforce the economic delusion that time is a resource we have at our disposal to be "used," as if there were a difference between "me" and "my time." Here-and-now therapeutic frameworks in this way serve as forums for arguing over whose experience of reality is to be accepted and whose is to be disqualified. This can only preclude symbolization and reduce the clinical relationship to an experience of transference as distortion, effectively putting the analyst in a position of authority and knowledge. In this way, here-and-now techniques reflect a form of treatment that bends itself to the demands of the consumer in order to accommodate for the calculated promises of determinable and specifiable goals.

When patient and analyst are each focused on the here-and-now in such a way that opposes their perspectives and that precludes symbolization on either of their parts, they are entrenched in what Birksted-Breen calls "a malignantly denuded present" (2003, p. 1503). This is a position of clinical impasse "which hinges on the reduction of time to the present" (p. 1505). To this reduction Birksted-Breen opposes the form of *thinking* that she sees as specific to clinical practice. Symbolization is a form of thinking that grasps that what things presently appear to be is not necessarily what they are. On the part of the analyst this kind of thinking is conceived as evenly suspended attention or reverie, while on the part of the patient this kind of thinking elaborates itself as free association. These practices together indicate a form of thinking-as-relation that is not that of the cognitive or representational-calculative valorization of causal, conscious connection.[2] For Birksted-Breen, the form of thinking intrinsic to the analytic experience is one that symbolizes, not one that consciously explains; it traces enduring paths without orienting itself toward the goal of providing immediate solutions. With reference to Bion, she writes:

> Paradoxically, being 'without memory and desire', which suspends chronological time (past and future), enables a different temporality to predominate, *the non-chronological time of reverie* and one that creates a necessary *temporal space* within the analytic situation. It is opposite to an orientation to goals, which includes the goal of promoting symbolization.
>
> (2012, p. 827; emphases added)

To be without memory and desire—to occupy the position of analytic neutrality, the capacity to demonstrate which is central to formation as an analyst—is not to exist purely in the moment, but to inhabit a different temporality or temporal space in which the immediacy of the intersubjective encounter is no longer privileged, and in which adaptation to the demands of the Other (i.e. symptom reduction) is no longer a therapeutic goal. Contrary to what some authors who have taken up Bion's description of the analytic stance would have us believe, there is nothing either mystical or formally unattainable about this ideal. It is a thoroughly attainable, rigorously materialist position, yet one altogether at odds with the ways in which we are encouraged to think and to behave as consumers entrenched in the demands of the marketplace.[3]

The "double register" of clinical "reverberation time"—what we might call, bringing Loewald to bear on this point, the ecstatic time of clinical resonance—is what Birksted-Breen develops as "the time of suspended attention, reverie and mental digestion, on which is based the back and forth between patient and analyst" (2012, p. 820). The "back and forth" she is referring to is not an intersubjective exchange but what occurs when one participant openly associates while the other floats freely, attempting together to abandon the position of the subject as well as the logical and dialectical rules that govern ordinary discourse. This reverberating back and forth in "the time of suspended attention, reverie and mental digestion" recalls Loewald's "differentiating processes... conceptualized as primary internalizations and externalizations," which he had symbolized, like Derrida, in terms of reading and writing. Recall also Derrida's claim, "there is only tele-analysis, they will have to draw all the conclusions as we do, get their concept of the 'analytic situation' *to swallow a new metrics of time*." As if communicating with while remaining completely unaware of key Derridean texts such as *Glas* (1990) and "Tympan" (1982a), themselves grounded in Heidegger's theme of the "call"

**88** A new metrics of clinical time

in *Being and Time* (1996) and in *What is Called Thinking?* (1968), Birksted-Breen elaborates the metaphor of "reverberation" as describing a form of material communication prior to the voice and to speech. In passing she describes this as, "…a more primitive experience of connectiveness" (2012, p. 831), one grounded in the body and that provides "access [to] that which lies beyond the mnemic trace" (p. 830). Such access demands that we revise our conception of the relationship between mind and environment as a relationship between a subject and a series of objects. As Heidegger had argued, such a relationship cannot properly constitute a phenomenologically meaningful world. The psychoanalytic clinic provides us with a situation in which this framework wields limited explanatory power, and in which this power threatens to function defensively as a means of clinging to a desymbolizing, oppositional logic:

> Architecturally, reverberation describes the way sound travels back in modified form after coming up against a surface. It accounts for the echo. 'Reverberate' is akin to the word 'resonate' which is used metaphorically to describe the attunement of one person to another person's meaning. Reverberation, the echo, describes *an ill-defined area between narcissism and object relation*, and is thus appropriate for the earliest mother and infant experiences. It is, in Winnicott's terms, a transitional space. The infant sees himself in his mother's face as Winnicott … describes in his notion of the mother as mirror, or, one could add, hears himself in her sound response to the sounds he produces. But the mother is not like a physical mirror which would just reproduce mechanically. The mother brings herself, her feelings, her unconscious into the interaction, so that transformation is always taking place. In that sense, in my view there is no clear delineation between primary narcissism and primitive object relation.
>
> (2009, pp. 39–40; emphasis in original)

Like the word "resonance," Birksted-Breen's "reverberation" is intended as a metaphor for describing "the attunement of one person to another person's meaning." Derrida, whose expanded notion of writing describes precisely this sharing of meaning prior to language as speech, would have us ask: If resonance and reverberation insistently suggest themselves across texts by disparate authors as metaphors for attunement, then what exactly does attunement mean, and why does it consistently evoke this supplementary vocabulary of resonance, reverberation and echo? What accounts for the intuitive coherence of the metaphor of attunement? Is the harmonizing function of attunement only a metaphor, or does it rather describe accurately the way in which minds or brains interact with one another nonmetaphysically? What kind of space is being traversed by this echoing attunement, and what does it mean for an individual mind-brain apparatus to "tune in" to another, or for two such apparatuses to tune in to the same wavelength, like old radios dialing in some distant and ghostly signal?

"*An ill-defined area between narcissism and object relation*" indicates that whatever attunement consists in, it concerns an area in which the absolute opposition between

A new metrics of clinical time **89**

subjectivity and objectivity no longer holds. Although her general orientation is Kleinian, when running up against the limitations of this metaphysical framework Birksted-Breen consistently invokes Winnicott: "Psychoanalysis, one could say, operates in that 'transitional space' which is the ambiguous play between temporalities" (2009, p. 37). She allows us to appreciate the extent to which Winnicott's reflections on transitional phenomena, dynamically not-me possessions, and potential space-time are indebted to Freud's reflections on unconscious communication as "technological" telepathy. If there is a space and time of unconscious, "telepathic" communication it is the potential space-time that Winnicott challenges us to think in terms of transitionality—a term that functions at the border and in excess of contemporary metaphysics *qua* cognitive science. What cognitive science as a form of representational-calculative thinking defends against is what Birksted-Breen calls reverberation time, what Winnicott called transitional phenomena, as these are intrinsic to what Heidegger called thinking and to what Derrida called writing.[4] These concepts are not mutually reducible, but each indicates a complex, open (temporal) relation to the other that provokes anxious efforts to shut down symbolic awareness in favor of fact-minded, authoritarian orientations toward the exclusive "reality" of the here-and-now.

In the above quoted passage, at the very moment that she defers to Winnicott, Birksted-Breen encounters the limitations of Winnicott's approach as these are symptomatically condensed in the analogy of the mirror—an analogy that is, of course, in no way specific to Winnicott. The mother as primitive mirroring technology is not just a technology of the visual image but of the auditory voice, of the body as a form of relational technology rather than as something that is ever merely present in an idealized sense: "And the telematic *tekhne* is not a paradigm or materialized example of another thing, *it is that* (compare our mystic writing pad, it is an analogous problematic, it all communicates by telephone)" (Derrida 2007, p. 242). The mutual presence of bodies does not merely facilitate communication via the voice in the form of language as speech. Rather, the presence of speaking bodies, as distilled by the analytic situation—a situation that is not contained spatially by the room but by the frame that insists as the transitional space-time of repetition in returning—emphasizes the ecstatic yet concealed dimension of speech as writing: the "reverberation time" of the "echo" that indicates the non-sensuous, "spiritual" materiality of auto-hetero-affection.

When Birksted-Breen writes, "But the mother is not like a physical mirror which would just reproduce mechanically. The mother brings herself, her feelings, her unconscious into the interaction, so that transformation is always taking place," it seems as if her effort is to abandon the technological metaphor of the mirror-mother in favor of an empathic, humanist mother whose narcissistically all-powerful feelings would appear to embody the essence of the "living present." However, what she indicates is the extent to which technical metaphors are irreducible at the very moment that one wishes to dispense with them and to insist on maternal care as the embodiment of spontaneity and freedom. Unlike so many authors in the field, Birksted-Breen recognizes this constraint and chooses not to reduce it towards

**90** A new metrics of clinical time

yet another form of cognitive opposition: "in my view there is no clear delineation between primary narcissism and primitive object relation." As a result, she arrives at a conception of psychoanalysis as a clinical effort at deconstructing the metaphysics of presence:

> All pathologies deal with problems to do with time and the inability to accept change, that is, a movement in time: fixation, regression, psychic retreat, repetition compulsion. Psychoanalysis itself can be used as such a timeless retreat. Mourning and melancholia typify the two opposite relationships to time. Vertical splits enable different parts of the personality to have different relationships to time, by which I mean that neurotic parts of the personality may function according to a notion of time passing, while psychotic parts of the personality function on the omnipotent stoppage of time passing.
>
> (2009, p. 39)

To put it in a formula: *psycho*pathology is *chrono*pathology. Versions of psychoanalysis that reject practices of reverie and that instead focus insistently on asserting interpretive control over the here-and-now of the transference inherently tend toward clinical impasse. Where the kind of *thinking* that both constitutes and is constituted by the matrix of the analyst in reverie and the patient engaged in free association— a matrix that is more than a merely intersubjective dialogue, as a form of non-metaphysical, open relation—is in play, interpretation functions as a way of modifying chronopathological structures. Such modification involves a practice of interpretation as something other than causal explanation, as an effort at cultivating open pathways for potential transformation and change. Interpretation as a way of intervening at the level of the ecstatic, non-causal "echo" would be an effort to demonstrate an articulated (technical) structure—what Heidegger had called care (*Sorge*)—that cannot be conceived in terms of a "clear delineation" between subjects and objects. Instead of conceiving subjects and objects spatially as essentially self-present or self-identical beings, the analytic experience of resonance or of reverberation time indicates an openness of self and other disclosed in the element of repetition:

> The task of psychoanalysis is, *via repetition,* to enable an unblocking of a present frozen in the past onto a possible future of open possibilities. A *new sense of time* is almost always mentioned, in my experience, by patients in the latter phases of their analyses, a new sense of time *which has been mediated by the analyst's psyche* in the interchange between patient and analyst.
>
> (p. 39; emphases added)

The crucial insight here, what links Birksted-Breen's approach to the "technological" dimension of deconstruction as a project beyond humanist appeals to the spontaneity of the living present, is her understanding of the essential role of repetition as this constructs and is constructed by the clinical frame as a form of transitional between. By situating temporality as repetition at the heart of the analytic process, Birksted-Breen emphasizes the technical conditions that allow for the emergence of reverberation time as the "telepathic" interaction between the unconscious of the patient and that of the analyst. Without the repetitive, mechanical nature of the analytic process—again: coming to the same place, at the same time, day after day—analyst and patient would not find opportunity for resonance or reverberation. This sounds banal but it is not: it is not simply because the analyst and patient spend so much time together that they naturally draw closer in the element of mutual understanding as a result of the relational dialogue. Rather, the analyst's neutral-interpretive stance, as based in freely floating attention—about which Birksted-Breen writes, "Such a state of mind implies a *withholding of immediate response and thus a duration*"—coupled with the repetitive nature of the clinical frame, allows for the modification of temporally dedifferentiated, chronopathological structures by opening up the temporal space necessary for symbolization. This is to "retroactively discover" a lost and concealed opening capable of rescuing the analytic relationship from the impasse of the here-and-now intrinsic to both psychopathology and metaphysics.

In stating that these modifications provide "a new sense of time which has been mediated by the analyst's psyche," Birksted-Breen indicates something rather more complex than the Freudian theme of communication between one subjective unconscious and another. In conceiving a "telepathic" form of communication that bypasses conscious awareness in such a way that can only be reconstructed or retrospectively discovered, Freud had done a great deal to challenge a classical metaphysics of subjectivity. But Freud and most authors who have subsequently taken up his reflections on this point have remained within a thinking of communication figured by a metaphysics of presence—a failure to think time and space ecstatically as forms of relation, so that communicating can only appear as something a subject does to an object.

What Birksted-Breen elaborates, though perhaps without fully grasping the implications of the more radical edge of her thinking, is a kind of "telepathic" temporality disclosed in repetition, in which transmission transforms what receives, and reception transforms what transmits.[5] This is what it means to state that, "the telepathic process would be physical in itself, except at its two extremes." This is not telepathy in the ordinary, absurd sense of some unique cognitive or precognitive psychological ability to observe the contents of other people's minds. What is at issue are rather unpredictable structures of repetition intrinsic to space and time themselves, and that open each onto the other in ways that make possible the transmission of meaning even in the absence of the living presence of speaking beings. This non-sensuous, intermediate material structure is ecstatic time as arche-writing, trace or différance, manifest spectrally as the transitional space-time of the analytic frame in its open-repetitive, relational-mechanical ("neutral") technicity.

## Notes

1 Although my consideration of Bollas here is rather brief, it could be argued quite cogently that no prominent contemporary clinical theorist has been more touched by Derrida's

**92** A new metrics of clinical time

influence than Bollas himself, to the point where an investigation of the relationship between Bollas's thought and deconstruction would require its own separate volume. At times Bollas is quite forthcoming about this influence, citing Derrida explicitly (Bollas 1992, pp. 63–64), while at other moments the unacknowledged reliance on Derridean themes is so overwhelming to the informed reader that one wonders if Bollas is deliberately concealing this influence in order not to have to deal with the justifications such an inheritance unfortunately tends to involve. Bollas received academic training in comparative literature at the State University of New York at Buffalo, where Derrida's work received some of its strongest early support. This in itself might be enough to indicate that references to "deconstruction" (2007, p. 5), to "dissemination" (1992, p. 68; 2007, p. 92; 2009, p. 10, p. 108), to "traces" (1992, p. 59; 2009, p. 87) and "temporal inscription" (2009, p. 88), to a "pre-verbal sphinx mother, silenced by language" (2000, p. 35) are not neutral with respect to Derrida's influence. To be clear, in no way am I suggesting that Bollas inappropriately credits himself with having invented these terms. Rather it is in his texts that we can read the traces of an inheritance that the author has risked preserving against a potential backlash by those readers easily triggered to mindless antagonism by the word "deconstruction." In any case, I do not believe it accidental that it took someone academically trained in comparative literature to accomplish something as important as what Bollas has accomplished in having retrieved the specifically Freudian clinical practices of free association and evenly suspended attention, and as a way of redressing the fixation on the here-and-now of so much contemporary psychoanalysis.

2  Readers familiar with the contemporary psychoanalytic literature will likely ask questions here about the relationship between what these authors are considering and Thomas Ogden's influential concept of the "analytic third." Ogden, whose early work I treated in Chapter 1, but whose later orientation I have deliberately chosen to defer commentary on, is unquestionably a thinker at the cutting edge of contemporary psychoanalytic thought where, as the central argument of the present text indicates, psychoanalysis intersects with the concerns and insights of deconstruction (he is yet another author for whom "resonance" is a crucial term [see Ogden 1996, p. 891]). However, as I remarked in Chapter 2, what this emergent discourse treats is something that cannot be figured in dialectical terms, suggesting something in excess of a classical dialectical logic. Ogden's insistent appeal to concepts like intersubjectivity and co-construction unfortunately, for me, tend to hinder and to obscure the more progressive and challenging insights that his reflections on the nature of the analytic process clearly have to offer. Frequently citing Winnicott on analysis as an "overlap between two areas of playing," Ogden nevertheless consistently returns us to a thinking in terms of the primacy of the self-enclosed, Cartesian subject. What the notion of the analytic third intends to describe would seem rather to take us beyond a Hegelian thematics of intersubjectivity and to open up instead a deconstructive—and properly Freudian—thinking about unconscious, non-subjective processes.

3  "Ultimately," writes Antonino Ferro (2011), "Bion's notorious phrase 'without memory or desire' means that each time we can begin anew with what we do not know, *avoiding excessive insistence on what we have already acquired*" (p. 99; emphasis added). Ferro is referring to the knowledge that the analyst acquires about the patient over the course of treatment, as well as the theoretical knowledge acquired while training as an analyst. Like Bion, he is implicitly criticizing an experiential organization of time that idealizes the "now" by prioritizing the possession of objects (answers) at the expense of development and future possibility (thinking). What Birksted-Breen calls "the non-chronological time of reverie" constitutes a form of resistance to the addictogenic here-and-now time of consumption that insists excessively on acquisition, that wants to be done quickly, and that attempts to

calculate all returns on its investments in advance. Psychoanalysis intrinsically involves cultivating this resistance.

4 Throughout her writings, Birksted-Breen often defers to "French psychoanalysis," by which she predominantly seems to mean the work of André Green and Jean Laplanche. She carefully avoids Lacan, while noting his pervasive influence. What she does not recognize is the extent to which these authors were influenced significantly by Derrida, especially in those aspects of their work that she draws upon.

5 Perhaps not surprisingly, it was Winnicott who first appreciated this deeper dimension of Freud's insight concerning unconscious communication in his essay, "Hate in the Countertransference" (1949). On this point, see Fabozzi (2012).

## References

Birksted-Breen, D. (2003). "Time and the *après-coup*." *International Journal of Psycho-Analysis*, 84: 1501–1515.

Birksted-Breen, D. (2009). "'Reverberation Time', Dreaming and the Capacity to Dream." *International Journal of Psycho-Analysis*, 90: 35–51.

Birksted-Breen, D. (2012). "Taking Time: The Tempo of Psychoanalysis." *International Journal of Psycho-Analysis*, 93: 819–835.

Bollas, C. (1992). *Being a Character: Psychoanalysis and Self Experience*. New York: Routledge.

Bollas, C. (2000). *Hysteria*. New York: Routledge.

Bollas, C. (2002). *Free Association*. Duxford, Cambridge: Icon.

Bollas, C. (2007). *The Freudian Moment*. London: Karnac.

Bollas, C. (2009). *The Evocative Object World*. New York: Routledge.

Derrida, J. (1976). *Of Grammatology*. Trans. G. Spivak. Baltimore, MD: Johns Hopkins University Press.

Derrida, J. (1982a). "Tympan." In: *Margins—Of Philosophy*. Trans. A. Bass Chicago, IL: University of Chicago Press. Pp. ix–xxix.

Derrida, J. (1982b). "Différance." In: *Margins—Of Philosophy*. Trans. A. Bass. Chicago, IL: University of Chicago Press. Pp. 3–27.

Derrida, J. (1990). *Glas*. Trans. J. P. Leavey and R. Rand. Lincoln, NE: University of Nebraska Press.

Derrida, J. (1998). *Resistances of Psychoanalysis*. Trans. P. Kamuf, P.-A. Brault, and M. Naas. Stanford, CA: Stanford University Press.

Derrida, J. (2007). "Telepathy." In: *Psyche: Inventions of the Other, Volume 1*. Ed. P. Kamuf and E. Rottenberg. Stanford, CA: Stanford University Press. Pp. 226–261.

Derrida, J. (2010). *Copy, Archive, Signature: A Conversation on Photography* Ed., G. Richter; trans. J. Fort. Stanford, CA: Stanford University Press.

Fabozzi, P. (2012). "A silent yet radical future revolution: Winnicott's innovative perspective." *Psychoanalytic Quarterly*, 81(3): 601–626.

Ferro, A. (2011). Shuttles to and from the unconscious. *The Italian Psychoanalytic Annual*, 5: 89–106.

Freedman, N. (1998). Psychoanalysis and symbolization: legacy or heresy? In: *The Modern Freudians: Contemporary Psychoanalytic Technique*. Ed. C. Ellman, S. Grand, M. Silvan, and S. Ellman. Northvale, NJ: Jason Aronson.

Freedman, N., & Lavender, J. (2002). On desymbolization: the concept and observations on anorexia and bulimia. *Psychoanalysis and Contemporary Thought*, 25: 165–200.

Freedman, N., & Russell, J.. (2003). "Symbolization of the analytic discourse." *Psychoanalysis and Contemporary Thought*, 26(1): 39–87.

## 94 A new metrics of clinical time

Freud, S. (1912). "Recommendations to physicians practicing psycho-analysis." S.E. 12.

Heidegger, M. (1968). *What is Called Thinking?* Trans. J. Glenn Gray. New York: Harper Perennial.

Heidegger, M. (1990). *Kant and the Problem of Metaphysics*. Trans. R. Taft. Bloomington, IN: Indiana University Press.

Heidegger, M. (1993). "Letter on Humanism." In: *Basic Writings*. Ed. D. Farrell Krell. New York: Harper and Row. Pp. 213–266.

Heidegger, M. (1996). *Being and Time*. Trans. J. Stambaugh. Albany, NY: SUNY Press.

Heidegger, M. (2002). "The end of philosophy and the task of thinking." In: *On Time and Being*. Trans. J. Stambaugh. Chicago, IL: University of Chicago Press. Pp. 55–73.

Heidegger, M. (2013). "Language." In: *Poetry, Language, Thought*. Trans. A. Hofstader. New York: Harper Perennial. Pp. 185–208.

Ogden, T. (1996). "Reconsidering Three Aspects of Psychoanalytic Technique." *International Journal of Psycho-analysis*, 77: 883–899.

Winnicott, D.W. (1949). "Hate in the Counter-transference." *International Journal of Psycho-Analysis*, 30: 69–74.

# 4

# PSYCHOANALYSIS AND PHARMACOLOGY

In *The Sickness Unto Death,* Kierkegaard writes, "As is natural, the world generally has no understanding of what is truly appalling" (1980, p. 34). What is natural, what is general, what can be understood and what is appalling are related in ways that do not conform to our everyday expectations. Kierkegaard indicates that this failure informs a certain experience of "the world generally." The general world is not the world lived experientially, it is the predictable world that provides few opportunities for becoming interested and invested in what is going on—an objective world that one imagines one "has." The difference between these worlds or between world and worldlessness was that to which Kierkegaard for the most part of his life addressed himself. Considering seriously the general program of the "leveling down process" (Kierkegaard 1962) that describes the modern world can only lead to a confrontation with that which is "truly appalling."

In his essay, "The Question Concerning Technology" (*Die Frage nach der Technik,* which might better be translated, "The Question of Technics"), Heidegger famously writes, "Because the essence of technology is nothing technological, essential reflection upon technology and decisive confrontation with it must happen in a realm that is, on the one hand, akin to the essence of technology and, on the other, fundamentally different from it" (1977, p. 35). Again it is a question of a fundamental difference between "realms," and Heidegger even more dramatically than Kierkegaard describes this relation as an uncircumventible "decisive confrontation." The topic of this confrontation is something that is itself "fundamentally different" and that as such does not respect anything that claims to be absolutely necessary or fundamental. Heidegger himself did not escape the pull to refuse this difference, but both he and Kierkegaard before him would have us believe that this is not a failure of any individual's thinking so much as a failure intrinsic to thinking itself.

The intention of this concluding chapter is to demonstrate the extent to which Kierkegaard's and Heidegger's claims and the economies they describe are identical

**96** Psychoanalysis and pharmacology

to one another. My effort will also be to open up the arguments hitherto pursued concerning the nature of the analytic clinic to social concerns which, as I have already indicated in previous chapters, are not outside or opposed to clinical thinking. Responding to the challenges of the contemporary world—challenges described by both Kierkegaard and Heidegger in terms of the dissolution of what historically and traditionally binds us together, as against the encroachment of the general—is made possible by the experience of the psychoanalytic clinic as "a realm that is, on the one hand, akin to the essence of technology and, on the other, fundamentally different from it."

## Clinic and technics

To say that "the essence of technology is nothing technological" is to indicate that efforts to think the relationship between the human and the technological cannot themselves be determined by a form of thinking that from the outset has been figured technologically. Elsewhere Heidegger (1966) distinguishes between what he calls "contemplative" or "meditative" thinking (his privileged example is poetry) and what he calls the "representational" or "calculative" thinking that has become predominant in the modern age. For Heidegger this technological form of thinking today insists on the irreducible character of the inner subject as it confronts a world of external objects, both of which stand in a relation of absolute opposition to the other. Wherever we find ourselves thinking in terms of an absolute opposition between the subjective and the objective, wherever we conceive of ourselves essentially as inner subjects whose central claim is their ability to manipulate outer objects, exercising domination over the natural world—that is, wherever the metaphysical project that has long dominated and controlled the destiny of the Western tradition continues to manifest itself—we are already thinking within a framework overdetermined by the demand that we submit ourselves to instrumental rationality.

This is why, for Heidegger, the worst way to approach the pathologies of the modern age would be to continue to think of technological objects as neutral tools that we merely use in our otherwise non-technical, spontaneous, everyday lives, and that receive their value from whether this neutral instrumentality is morally oriented toward either good or bad ends. This position assumes that human beings are not continuously and radically transformed by living immersed in a hyper-technological environment; it supposes an unchanging human essence capable of celebrating itself in the act of subjugating nature to the immediacy of its universal and therefore inherently justifiable demands. This is the collective fantasy that drives an era in which calculation replaces decision-making, the algorithmic having subsumed the place of symbolic thought. For Heidegger, the humanist celebration of subjectivity is not the alternative to, but the very essence of calculative, instrumental reason. To say that "the essence of technology is nothing technological" is at the same time to question whether the essence of humanity is itself something human in an ordinary, metaphysical sense. This is also to indicate that sensitivity to what is appalling is in no way natural—that it must be cultivated, technically.

Beginning with, yet in crucial ways departing from Heidegger's thinking about the necessity of a "confrontation" between the human and the technological, Derrida had seen that, to the extent that he poses the question of this relationship as a form of confrontation or opposition, thereby disavowing the essential role of the technical in the cultivation of human being or *Da-sein*, Heidegger had remained uncritically bound to the metaphysical tradition that his thinking otherwise worked so powerfully to deconstruct. In the name of an impossible science of grammatology—that is, at the limits of scientific thinking, and as a rigorous meditation on the very possibility of science as the transmission of ideality—Derrida had proposed the critical project of deconstruction as an alternative to a metaphysical logic capable of thinking only in terms of a binary opposition between technology's positive *or* negative effects. Autonomy and freedom are instead both made possible *and* threatened by the technical dimension of organic human life. To grasp this is to recognize that there is no humanity in the absence of our technological self-articulation. To imagine human beings in the absence of technological support is to remain bound to a religious perspective—to posit an Eden of innocence and a fall from a purely natural origin—one that begins as a naive anti-technology stance and that quickly devolves into a pogrom (as Heidegger was reluctant to discover). Technics—a term intended to encompass both technology and technique, art or craft like the ancient Greek word *tehknē*—inescapably and in every instance simultaneously compose and erode human relatedness. What we are witnessing today is a profoundly destabilizing acceleration of this tendency.

In *Civilization and Its Discontents*, Freud argues that industrial technologies make humanity into a "prosthetic God," one that "does not feel happy in his Godlike character" (1930, p. 92). Digital technologies and the inability to manage them exacerbate this condition into a pervasive, systemic misery that Western market democracies insistently celebrate as progress. Adam Curtis's BBC documentary series *Century of the Self* (2002) depicts this with admirable rigor and transparency. In the 1930s, Freud's nephew Edward Bernays had developed techniques of marketing that would allow American industries to manage mass markets that had emerged from the industrial manufacture of unnecessary products. American citizens had to be trained, via audio-visual advertising strategies, to adopt consumerism not only as an economic lifestyle but as a means of aesthetic self-expression. The citizen had to be re-educated about his or her political duty, by being made to believe that to exercise purchasing power is to contribute to the enhanced strength of the nation. The democratic state in turn became the sum of its subjects participating in the market as a form of free self-expression, and market deregulation would from then on appear as an enhancement of political freedom through the production of opportunities for consumption rendered as individual and collective choice. The promise here was that the more goods the marketplace provides us with, the greater becomes the register of human agency. Economic competition between privatized corporations thus appears as the superstructural expression of the spirit of progressive, historical freedom struggling to emancipate itself. Despite its unprecedentedly colossal failure, since 2016 the desire to continue investing in

**98** Psychoanalysis and pharmacology

this self-destructive fantasy has announced itself as the demand that we make ourselves "great again."

It would be easy to be condescending and to imagine that, to the extent that
we are witness to the emptiness and confusion intrinsic to this demand, we are
somehow capable of protecting ourselves from it. Given the nature of their clinical
work, analysts are in a position to appreciate how this desire in no way demarcates
an "us" from a "them," but rather how insidiously it corrodes any attempt to cultivate distinction and difference, leading to conditions of psychological suffering for
which people both seek out and are driven to ruin efforts to help and to care for
them. This is a historically immeasurable suffering that must be respected and clarified so that it can be recognized as shared.

## Clinical example

A patient initially came to me insisting that he did not need analysis, that his problem
is that he analyzes himself too much already. Gradually he made his way onto the
couch at three times a week, but he remains suspicious of my request that he simply
say whatever comes to mind without censoring his thoughts. He insists that our
task is to help him understand himself better, so that he can "get on with" his life.

The patient has just returned from a week's vacation in Jordan. He lays down,
pauses for a good two or three minutes, then he begins to marvel at what it's like
to experience an ancient culture, to witness "traces" (his word) of the passage of
nearly ten thousand years. Words fail him as he describes a profoundly "meditative" (again, his word) culture far removed from the accelerated pace of his career
in finance. Returning to the city is jarring, if not traumatic, and he is disturbed by
how quickly he finds himself reabsorbed into its relentless rhythm. He hasn't been
back but two days and already he feels himself moving at such an irresistible speed,
losing time, time which seemed to stretch out endlessly while he was away on
holiday in the desert.

He links his experience to our time spent working together. The analysis has
always seemed different to him than his time spent at work, yet he has never been
able shake the feeling that what we are doing together is itself a form of work, that
we need to produce results—that analysis too is like a job, like going to the gym
and keeping up with his friends and his numerous social media accounts. These
are tasks that burden him but that must be completed, to his satisfaction and to
the satisfaction of others—forms of satisfaction that are often difficult for him to
distinguish.

Jokingly, he hits on the idea that maybe my office is like a miniature version
of the Jordanian desert in a little corner of the electric urban sprawl that both
oppresses and sustains him, a space where time can stretch out and slow down. He
physically stretches out his body on the couch while he expresses this, and for a
moment he looks like a cat. He then says that he is beginning to sense that it is
acceptable for him just to lie there and be silent sometimes, that he doesn't have
to produce material for me to judge, which is so often synonymous with what he

imagines it means to engage in the analysis. Maybe to analyze and to judge oneself reflectively as if from the outside are not the same thing. Maybe this is different.

He says that he often has the strange sense in analysis, when he is recounting of the details of his past, that his childhood seemed to have lasted far longer than recent years, that in retrospect kindergarten through high school feels like it spanned decades. In contrast, having recently turned thirty, his twenties seem to have passed by in a flash. Being an adult involves another mindset, inhabiting a different "framework," he says. He wonders if there isn't a way to step out of this framework, to get back to the timing of his childhood, before work, before responsibility, before the pressure and the fear and the loneliness set in. The sense of nostalgia he generates is both poignant and exhausting.

Then, all of a sudden, he imagines that I have the key to this procedure. His voice switching from reminiscence to interrogation, he asks me what are the necessary steps he should take to accomplish this goal—as if to say, "Enough of psychoanalysis, there must be a behavioral regimen you can recommend." Since this is not an unusual request coming from the patient, I suggest that the difficulty lies in the fact that the question as he poses it—the idea that there is a program, a series of instructions to follow, a formal, universal procedure that can be simply given to him—that this demand itself belongs to the very framework he so desperately wants to step out of.

In other words, the patient is asking for a profound transformation in his basic experience of himself and of the world. But when he asks, "So how do I do it?" he is entrenched in the very position that causes him so much suffering by splitting him off from the world and making him feel that his life is speeding by. He wants an immediate answer that will cure him of his symptom, but the compulsive intensity of that demand precisely *is* his symptom.

When he falls silent, I sense an immense and complex despair.

## Cheap enjoyment

The logic at work here in the patient's demand is the logic of the industrialized marketplace that Freud had described in *Civilization and Its Discontents* with regard to the miseries of the prosthetic God. Too often read superficially and dismissed as a simply "pessimistic" text—one concerned with sociological speculation and therefore outside properly analytic concerns—*Civilization and Its Discontents* is in reality a text of profound clinical insight that deserves to be read carefully by contemporary practitioners.

A major yet generally unacknowledged theme of the text is what Freud calls "techniques in the art of living" (p. 80). The orientation of such techniques is the shaping of individual and collective libidinal economies. Beyond isolation and conformity lie "methods of averting suffering…which seek to influence our own organism" (p. 77). The collective organization of such methods of auto-affective self-influence, which is to say practices that cultivate *both* individuality *and* collectivity, is precisely what civilization is for Freud. Unlike other species that simply

**100** Psychoanalysis and pharmacology

express their biological instincts, human beings are unique in that we are subject to this recursive structure whereby, in expressing ourselves libidinally, we attempt to modify ourselves libidinally. This recursive structure, Freud indicates, is technics— it *is* the relationship between the human and the technological that civilization instances. What exactly does this mean?

Freud first acknowledges that, "the crudest, but also the most effective among these methods of influence is the chemical one—intoxication" (p. 77). Intoxication—the deliberate embrace of that which is toxic—is something Freud laments science has not yet made a proper effort to understand:

> The service rendered by *intoxicating media* in the struggle for happiness and in keeping misery at a distance is so highly prized as a benefit that individuals and peoples alike have given them an established place in the economics of the libido. We owe to such media not merely the immediate yield of pleasure, but also a greatly desired degree of *independence from the external world*. For one knows that, with the help of this 'drowner of cares' one can at any time withdraw from the pressure of reality and find refuge in a world of one's own with better conditions of sensibility. As is well known, it is precisely this property of intoxicants which also determines their danger and injuriousness.
>
> (ibid.; emphases added)

The argument here is that we seek "independence from the external world"— individual autonomy—but in striving for this autonomy we reach for intoxicants that enhance our sense of autonomy in such a way that ruins our autonomy. We want to be free, but what immediately enhances our sense of freedom simultaneously ravages it. This is, of course, the logic of addiction, which Freud grasps is intimately linked (if not structurally identical) to the logic of autonomy itself. The longer it takes to become independent, the more frustrated we can become; yet the more quickly we obtain our independence, the more short-lived it can be. Frustrated by this illogical logic, we reach for intoxicating media. Attempting to care for ourselves without mediation—disavowing the irreducibly mediated, technical dimension of our ability to care both for ourselves and for one another—we drown our ability to care and we obliterate ourselves.

Beyond intoxicating media, Freud enumerates other techniques in the art of living—instinctual renunciation, hermetic withdrawal, delusional investment, love—all of which appear on some level to be further articulations of intoxicating media and all of which ultimately fail to provide satisfaction and to protect from pain. This is the "pessimistic" aspect upon which the text's reputation is built. But Freud's concern is not with affirming the objective truth of the insistence of what he calls "real misery" (p. 80). To the contrary, his concern is with understanding what it is that threatens and what it is that sustains this art of living which is at the heart of the massive technical apparatus that is civilization. What he indicates in several passages throughout the text is that what threatens this art of living, this essence of civilization that constitutes the possibility of our humanity, is in fact the very same thing that gives rise to it in the first place. The fullest discussion of this insight appears in Chapter 3, in a passage that is worth quoting at length:

> During the last few generations mankind has made an extraordinary advance in the natural sciences and in their technical application and has established his control over nature in a way never before imagined. The single steps of this advance are common knowledge and it is unnecessary to enumerate them. Men are proud of those achievements, and have a right to be. But they seem to have observed that this newly-won power over space and time, this subjugation of the forces of nature, which is the fulfillment of a longing that goes back thousands of years, has not increased the amount of pleasurable satisfaction which they may expect from life and has not made them feel happier. From the recognition of this fact we ought to be content to conclude that power over nature is not the *only* precondition of human happiness, just as it is not the *only* goal of cultural endeavor; we ought not to infer from it that technical progress is without value for the economics of our happiness. One would like to ask: is there, then, no positive gain in pleasure, no unequivocal increase in my feeling of happiness, if I can, as often as I please, hear the voice of a child of mine who is living hundreds of miles away or if I can learn in the shortest possible time after a friend has reached his destination that he has come through the long and difficult voyage unharmed? Does it mean nothing that medicine has succeeded in enormously reducing infant mortality and the danger of infection for women in childbirth, and, indeed, in considerably lengthening the average life of a civilized man? And there is a long list that might be added to benefits of this kind which we owe to the much-despised era of scientific and technical advances. But here the voice of pessimistic criticism makes itself heard and warns us that most of these satisfactions follow the model of the 'cheap enjoyment' extolled in the anecdote—the enjoyment obtained by putting a bare leg from under the bedclothes on a cold winter night and drawing it in again. If there had been no railway to conquer distances, my child would never have left his native town and I should need no telephone to hear his voice; if traveling across the ocean by ship had not been introduced, my friend would not have embarked on his sea-voyage and I should not need a cable to relieve my anxiety about him. What is the use of reducing infantile mortality when it is precisely that reduction which imposes the greatest restraint on us in the begetting of children, so that, taken all round, we nevertheless rear no more children than in the days before the reign of hygiene, while at the same time we have created difficult conditions for our sexual life in marriage, and have probably worked against the beneficial effects of natural selection? And, finally, what good to us is a long life if it is difficult and barren of joys, and if it is so full of misery that we can only welcome death as a deliverer?

> (pp. 86–87; emphases in original)

**102** Psychoanalysis and pharmacology

The paragraph begins with Freud's praise for the tremendous advances in the subjugation of nature that have occurred over the previous few generations, as a process dramatically accelerated by the subordination of science to the development of technology and as facilitating "this newly-won power over space and time." Even though we may not conclude that this power is all there is worth striving for, it would be foolish to deny that we are not in large measure better off—by which Freud means, from the perspective of an economics of libido, capable of experiencing greater enjoyment—under these circumstances than under conditions that for centuries actively worked to prevent the development of technology and of knowledge as technique (for preventing unnecessary death and for extending life, for example). Freud writes that he will not waste time considering the objections of those who conservatively reject the advancement of the sciences and of technology in principle (as "much-despised"). But he is willing to take seriously the "voice of pessimistic criticism" which sees in the advancement of the technical sciences not greater enjoyment but the proliferation of "cheap enjoyment."

Freud thus holds himself between conservative and progressive values: the advance of civilization both creates more enjoyment and at the same time cheapens that enjoyment and potentially ruins our capacity for enjoyment; we are living in much better times but we are unhappy for that very reason; the present is in many ways much better than the past, which was nonetheless in many ways much better than the present. Referring to the advent of mechanical and electrical tele-technologies, Freud asks, "is there, then, no positive gain in pleasure, no unequivocal increase in my feeling of happiness, if I can, as often as I please, hear the voice of a child of mine who is living hundreds of miles away or if I can learn in the shortest possible time after a friend has reached his destination that he has come through the long and difficult voyage unharmed?" Identifying with the "pessimistic" struggle he indicates that there is value in the response, "If there had been no railway to conquer distances, my child would never have left his native town and I should need no telephone to hear his voice."

Adducing other and more powerful examples, Freud elaborates this same logic whereby what enhances our autonomy and freedom is simultaneously what undercuts our autonomy and makes us more and more dependent. Failing to appreciate this paradox and instead oscillating between investment in either extreme results in "a gradual stupefying process, the cessation of expectations, and cruder or more refined methods of narcotization" that irreversibly alter our "receptivity to sensations of pleasure and unpleasure" (p. 88). What Freud sees is that what contemporary techno-science gives us with one hand, it compromises with the other; the capacity for intelligence that it supports and expands, it simultaneously undermines and destroys. There is no way to step outside of this paradox, no great era that did not live out this struggle to which we might return. We must learn to live within this paradox more deeply and with greater awareness by cultivating *techniques* in the art of living. What deflects this effort from our ability to think sufficiently about this situation is the temptation immediately to ask, like the patient in the example provided above, "*So how do we do this?*" It is the automatic and impulsive quality

Psychoanalysis and pharmacology **103**

of this response that both Freud and Heidegger ask us to spend time with. To take time—to take *our* time, which is at the same time to take *one's own* time—in asking questions about why we are driven to ask certain questions and not others is what is meant most generally by philosophy.

Psychoanalysis today is in a unique position with regard to its diminishing yet still available status as an orientation of the contemporary mental health professions. Faced with a patient population that insistently demands positivist, instrumental approaches to solving psychological and behavioral problems, while simultaneously complaining that this demand itself and the compulsion to repeat it is relentlessly destroying their spirit, an analytic approach—which as I have tried to establish is determined less by its particular and often contradictory theories of human nature and of what is clinically mutative, and more by the intensively repetitive, incalculable open-endedness of its technical frame as what authorizes an interpretive praxis that is not about plugging readymade solutions into diagnostically encapsulated problems—refuses to remain complicit with what ruins people's lives in order to convert their suffering into an exploitable resource for sustaining the profession. Rejecting manualized techniques and standardized treatment plans, psychoanalysis inherently and necessarily falls outside of and constitutes a form of resistance to the mental health industry as an industrialized response to the pathologies of industrialization. In contrast to other clinical approaches that rely upon and thereby reinforce the downward spiral of instrumental reason, psychoanalysis as a technique in the art of living potentially offers alternative ways of thinking about and experiencing the relationship between self and world. Or, as the patient in the example above so succinctly put it: "Maybe this is different."

## From Derrida's pharmacy to Stiegler's pharmacology

According to a famously pithy dismissal by the early twentieth-century critic Karl Kraus, "Psychoanalysis is the mental illness [*Geisteskrankheit*] of which it purports to be the cure" (cited in Grosskurth 1977, p. 17). As it is directed at the very activity by means of which they sustain themselves, analysts are likely to miss the profound insight that this charge contains. English-speaking clinicians are particularly apt to avoid the accusation as to their own "mental illness" without first feeling invited to reflect on the "spiritual sickness" (*Geisteskrankheit*) of which Kraus was writing, and for which the youth generation that read him at the time felt he was largely speaking not just to but *for* them. Kraus had managed to energize a young generation against authoritarianism by disclosing the logic according to which what purports to be the cure for a given era's spiritual sickness can in fact be an expression of what causes such sickness or malaise (Freud's *das Unbehagen*) to begin with. Among those that Kraus's condemnation inspired was a young Melanie Klein, who would go on to become the most influential psychoanalyst after Freud.

A sickness that is also its own cure will be a formula familiar to readers already versed in the critical resources of deconstruction. In his 1972 collection *Dissemination*, Derrida provided a critical reading of Plato's dialogue *Phaedrus*,

**104** Psychoanalysis and pharmacology

which until then had largely been considered by scholars as among Plato's least coherent works, belonging either to his earliest or to his latest period, and in either case to the margins of his canon. The *Phaedrus* seems rather chaotic in its efforts to draw together reflections on memory, writing, madness, the soul, desire and rhetoric. In his commentary on the dialogue, entitled "Plato's Pharmacy," Derrida demonstrated how the circulation of the signifier *pharmakon*—an undecidably ambiguous word that, like "drug," can mean either poison or remedy depending on the context in which it appears—made the meaning of the dialogue dependent upon the way in which the reader was predisposed to encounter and to interpret not just its argument but the very words by means of which the argument is constructed (in writing, without the possibility of consulting the author as to his original intention).

In the dialogue, Socrates conceives of writing as a *pharmakon*—a drug that can either support or destroy memory, or that can at the same time support *and* destroy memory, like the pharmaceutical that can cure us of one addiction while forming the basis for another. Recounting the Egyptian myth of Theuth, inventor of the technology of writing, Socrates argues that whereas it appears as if the ability to write enhances human memory, in truth it weakens human memory by making human beings increasingly dependent upon material inscription. It seems as if writing makes up for failures of memorization and increases mastery and independence, but in fact it accelerates those failures of memorization by making the human more and more dependent upon this technology which despite appearances is just as fragile as those biological substrates that it intends to supplement. As a technological exteriorization of memory, writing both preserves memory and exposes it to potentially greater risks and losses.

What Derrida's reading of the *Phaedrus* and of the sequence that the paradoxical double meaning of the word *pharmakon* operates within it had demonstrated—in terms provided by but ultimately in excess of a merely literary analysis—was that the meaning of Plato's text was entirely determined not by the author but by the position of the reader (concerning, for example, the moral status of intoxication or drug taking), and in ways that neither the reader nor the author were capable of fully accounting for or controlling. It was this gesture, which Derrida repeated across a series of texts once his reputation as a serious and formidable scholar had been established, that came to be identified with the meaning of the word "deconstruction." This identification would function for the remainder of Derrida's career as a sign that deconstruction was nothing more than an attempt to discredit the authority of tradition, a relativistic nihilism that sought to level all differences and to enforce a sense that anything goes in the critical domain. This is why critics unfamiliar with Derrida's actual writings have been able to sustain an attack on deconstruction long after its having fallen out of fashion in the university circuit.

What Derrida had identified as the logic of *pharmaka*—according to which what supplements or supports at the same time weakens, what cultivates at the same time undermines—was what Freud had contended with in attempting to think the paradoxes of autonomy from the perspective of an economics of libido. In a footnote added in 1931 to the conclusion of Chapter 2 of *Civilization and Its Discontents*, in which he attempts to update his conclusions concerning the irreducibility of suffering for a being whose independence is dependent upon its relation to others, Freud writes, "No discussion of the possibilities of human happiness should omit to take into consideration the relation between narcissism and object libido. We require to know *what being essentially self-dependent signifies for the economics of the libido*" (p. 84; emphasis added). Autonomy is a difficult phenomenon to account for from a perspective that insists on the primacy of the pleasure principle as a tendency towards energetic discharge. What "being essentially self-dependent signifies for the economics of the libido" would be something other than the primacy of the pleasure principle and of any solipsism indicated by an undivided and singular, self-present origin.

This was precisely Loewald's concern, as I discussed at the end of Chapter 2, when he investigated the irreducibility of "non-climactic processes" as the province of libidinal economies capable of sublimation. For Loewald, psychoanalysis must be able to account for such processes or risk abandoning its status as a scientific discipline: "If the libido theory … is abandoned—if, let us say, primacy of self, in contrast to primacy of libido, is stipulated—then the meaning of the concept of sublimation vanishes, to give way, perhaps, to a creationist view of the world" (Loewald 1988, p. 5). Writing from North America in the late 1980s, Loewald was clearly speaking out against the fact that this was exactly what had already happened in psychoanalysis, that it had renounced its scientific calling and had become yet another mouthpiece for a classical metaphysics (via self-psychology and what was becoming intersubjectivism, for which the concepts of libido and of the drive can only appear anachronistic). Freud appears to have anticipated this regressive turn, which is perhaps why he was amenable to the "voice of pessimistic criticism" that sees in merely supportive techniques an anti-analytic, disindividuating tendency. This does not align Freud with the authoritarianism historically practiced in his name, but it does align him with Derrida's efforts to outline a position that is at once capable of criticizing all claims to absolute authority while exercising an authorizing function in selecting for tendencies that sustain both collective and individual futures worth investing in.

Freud's effort in *Civilization and Its Discontents* is to outline an account of the civilizing process, which is to say of the history of the relationship between (biological) human beings and the (technological) means by which they sustain themselves as (ethical) human beings by economizing libidinal dynamics into stable structures that can be maintained and that prove transmissible over generational time. These structures operate according to what Bernard Stiegler, drawing on Derrida's analysis of the Platonic *pharmakon* that is writing, provocatively describes as a *pharmacology*—an undecidable logic where the needed remedy is also the poison that generates the need—thereby appropriating and attempting to transform the discourse of an industry that advertises the cheap enjoyment of happiness as endless chemical dependency and consumption. The pharmacological situation of the human being

**106** Psychoanalysis and pharmacology

is what exposes it at once to sublimation through practices of creativity, and to self-destruction through tendencies toward addiction.

Stiegler's efforts to outline a pharmacology of contemporary technics—as a developmental account of the historical forms that collective libidinal economies assume, as lived techniques of relating human beings and the technological support systems that maintain their relations with one another (Freud's "art of living," or what Aristotle had called *politics*)—is not limited to an analysis of cultural formations. Stiegler takes seriously the Heideggerian question of technics in its original, onto-logical orientation as an existential analytic or as a practical question concerning the ways in which we lead our everyday lives. The orientation of this renewal or this reinvestment that is at once a fundamental critique proceeds along lines opened by Derrida in terms of a pharmacology of being that thinks the relationship—non-metaphysically conceived, as other than an instrumental account of a subject's rela-tion to an object—between the human and the technical, which is to say between the living and the dead, between the living presence of the voice and the dead letter of the written, or between life as it is now and the irretrievable past in the form of a tension or *binding* that makes us feel—as a form of resistance to the voice of pessimism, which can become suicidal—that life is worth living, even when we are radically unsure of what is to come.

In an early review of Stiegler's *Technics and Time, Volume One: The Fault of Epimetheus*, translator Richard Beardsworth parenthetically expressed a "serious regret" over the book's "lack of a confrontation between its thinking of memory and inheritance and Freud's theory of the unconscious" (1995, p. 89). Noting that such a confrontation would have been too complex at such an initial juncture, Beardsworth nevertheless promised that Stiegler "has at the very least opened up a major field of inquiry for the future theoretical work of psychoanalysis." As Stiegler's project has since taken to incorporating an increasingly broad psychoanalytic point of reference, now would seem to be an appropriate moment to open up this field of inquiry from the side of psychoanalysis itself. Taking into account what it means for psychoanalysis to be both a theory of human nature and a clinical practice that challenges any essentialist determinations of that nature, Stiegler's philosophical output allows psy-choanalysis to appreciate what it means that its theoretical framework can function at once as a practical, therapeutic technique of individuation.

The "major field of inquiry" Stiegler opens up for the theoretical work of psy-choanalysis pre-eminently concerns the future of analytic practice. By offering new ways of configuring the relationship between theory and practice that are not determined by the founding philosophical gesture that opposes the empir-ical and the transcendental or the material and the ideal, the most pressing import of Stiegler's work for psychoanalysis may be its ability to facilitate a powerful response to the challenges that its clinic faces today with regard to what, with a nod to Marcuse (2002), constitutes the "total administration" of the mental health industry. Situating psychoanalysis in relation to what Heidegger in *Being and Time* calls the modern technological "wish-world," in which "what is available … is *never enough*" (1996, p. 182; emphasis added), is an urgent task. Stiegler's approach to this wish-world—a world defined by its commitment to modalities of care-less addiction—updates and critically transforms Heidegger's understanding of Da-sein's ontological care-structure by integrating it with, rather than opposing it to, the question concerning technology. It is within a general thematics of technics *qua pharmaka* (both poison and remedy), and through a reconsideration of the meaning of therapeutic technique, that psychoanalysis today must respond to the demands of a patient population addicted to the bureaucratized passivity of "managed care."

Throughout the remainder of the chapter, beginning with a reading of paragraph 41 of *Being and Time*, I will develop how Heidegger's project for a fundamental ontology is elaborated by Stiegler in terms of the material inscription of "spirit" in ways that open onto a viable future for thinking the practical consequences of any approach to the Freudian unconscious. As Stiegler describes, the wish-world today—in which even those who are not addicted (to drugs, alcohol, television, etc.) become addicted to efforts at not being addicted (via pharmaceuticals, corrective behavioral and dietary regimens, "lifecoaching," etc.)—consists in the proliferation of *pharmaka* that promote new addictions to resisting addiction, often worsening the trends they purport to combat. Psychoanalysis is the only form of therapeutic engagement whose trace remains recognizable in—yet in such a way that proves it cannot be thoroughly co-opted by—the busy marketplace of currently available therapies, and that is capable of understanding and responding to the global crisis of care that Stiegler has prolifically dedicated himself to diagnosing.

## Fundamental ontology interprets care

The climactic disclosure of ecstatic temporality as Da-sein's "articulated care struc-ture"—being-ahead-of-itself (future) as already-being-in (past) as being-together-with (present)—occurs in Paragraph 41 of *Being and Time*. This disclosure opens immediately onto Heidegger's analyses of wishing, willing, urge and addiction. In offering up an analysis of these modalities of being, Heidegger is describing the modern technological world, which enforces tranquilization through absorption in the real. What is at issue here is the meaning of the emergence of a culture of absolute consumption, a "wish-world": "Being-in-the-world whose world is pri-marily projected as a wish-world has lost itself utterly in what is available, but in such a way that in the light of what is wished for, what is available (all the things at hand) is never enough" (p. 182). The proximity of Heidegger's critique of the wish-world to the disclosure of the meaning of being as time suggests that funda-mental ontology—as the practice conceived of by the early Heidegger, beyond the horizon of Husserlian phenomenology—is to be approached as an immanently social, political project.

Where Heidegger discusses wishing, this is about a kind of anticipation that refuses possibility: wishing wishes for something to be objectively present-at-hand. Wishing, willing, urge and addiction are further specifications of Da-sein's falling away from itself towards objective presence, in an effort to suppress anxiety over being-in-the-world. The wish-world is the world of the eminently actual, which

**108** Psychoanalysis and pharmacology

actively discredits the reality of the possible. The world driven by technological and economic innovation organizes itself in terms of actuality. The wish-world is driven to actualize the real, fleeing the reality of the possible. Heidegger's project for a fundamental ontology is interested in reality, not the real: "The leveling down of the possibilities of Da-sein to what is initially available in an everyday way at the same time results in a phasing out of the possible as such. The average everydayness of taking care of things becomes blind to possibility and gets tranquilized with what is merely 'real'" (pp. 181–182). For Heidegger, the real is not something that escapes Da-sein as some thing-in-itself; rather, the real describes the ontical reduction of reality as dynamic process to the managerial regulation of beings isolated from one another in objective presence.

Heidegger's argument here is twofold. First, he is arguing that care is more basic to our being, it is more "primordial," in that, unlike wishing and willing, care is not an activity but an ontological structure. Although, as for Freud and Nietzsche (whom Heidegger likely does not specifically have in mind), wishing and willing can be conceived as activities that condition and that allow for the emergence of the subject, these are nevertheless activities—they are doings, not beings, regardless as to who or what is doing the wishing or willing (i.e. the unconscious, the body, etc.). Care is prior to this determination, it describes what makes these actualities possible.

Secondly, Heidegger indicates that the world that constitutes itself in terms of wishing and willing as a relentless pursuit of the actual is itself a figure of care. According to an existential analytic, the modern technological wish-world is not opposed to care—it *is* care, ontically or "inauthentically" determined. When we act willingly and wishfully, we disclose our being as care, but in such a way that this is consistently covered over and forgotten. The relationship between self (defined in terms of its capacity for wishing and willing, whether consciously or unconsciously) and world (defined as a totality of regions in which mastery always might be exercised) emerges as the subject/object structure that insistently works to conceal our being-in-the-world *as* care and as something not that we *do* but that we *are*. That the being of Da-sein is care realizes a complexity that exceeds what might be articulated in terms of the relationship between a subject and any activity it undertakes: "The whole of the constitution of Da-sein itself is not simple in its unity, but shows a structural articulation which is expressed in the existential concept of care" (p. 186). Wishing, willing, urge, addiction are all activities undertaken by a subject, performances carried out by an underlying being. Care, on the other hand, describes not an activity but the existence, the "being-there" of Da-sein as such.

According to *Being and Time*, the wish-world splits apart theory and practice, defining itself in terms of the effectiveness of this splitting. In doing so this world endlessly celebrates its ability to extract from itself an actuality that it is driven to prioritize over its being as possibility. This describes how the scientific spirit is betrayed in being reduced to the production of quantifiable, calculable results, and in such a way that not only encourages but that insists on statistical thinking as the measure of understanding and knowledge. This is precisely what the disclosure of being as care, around which the project for a fundamental ontology is organized, challenges:

> As a primordial structural totality, care lies "before" every factical "attitude" and "position" of Da-sein, that is, it is always already in them as an existential a priori. Thus this phenomenon by no means expresses a priority of "practical" over theoretical behavior. When we determine something objectively present by merely looking at it, this has the character of care just as much as a "political action," or resting and having a good time. "Theory" and "praxis" are possibilities of being for a being whose being must be defined as care.
>
> (p. 180)

Heidegger's fundamental ontology works toward a coincidence of theory and practice, an integration realized by means of an interpretive disclosure that is not "about" Da-sein but that is a working on or through the question of the meaning of being and that transforms human being in the process. In the absence of such an effort the political and the ethical are as a result split off as specific dimensions of action, where action is then opposed to thought determined as reflection and as abstraction from the priority of the real. Ethics and politics so conceived can only function as strategies for consumption and forgetfulness. Fundamental ontology works against this, as a counter-practice to the nihilism of the technological wish-world through descriptive disclosure of human being as care. This is why Paragraph 41 is taken up with both the interpretation of the being of Da-sein as articulated care structure, and the effort immediately to situate this interpretation with respect to subjectivity figured today in terms of its non-relational (narcissistic) tendencies towards wishing, willing, urge and addiction.

In *Kant and the Problem of Metaphysics* (1990), where fundamental ontology is conceived under the general heading of a "Metaphysics of Da-sein," Heidegger writes,

> The Metaphysics of Da-sein is not just metaphysics about Da-sein, but is the metaphysics which occurs necessarily *as Da-sein*. But for that reason: it can never become metaphysics "about" Da-sein, as for example zoology is about animals. The Metaphysics of Da-sein is no fixed and ready-for-use "organon" at all. It must always be built up anew amid the transformation of its idea in the working-out of the possibility of metaphysics.
>
> (p. 162; emphasis in original)

Heidegger is again arguing that fundamental ontology is not an abstract theory that represents or that is "about" being; rather it works with or on being, acting as a lever for changing the ways in which we *are* in our everyday lives. In this sense, the practice of fundamental ontology is more experimental than theoretical, and to the extent that it ultimately refuses or exceeds any such distinction between thought and experimental practice. We are effectively altering, transforming ourselves in

**110** Psychoanalysis and pharmacology

thinking like this, and to an extent that any opposition between thought and action is no longer tenable. Thinking being is something other than the activity of an underlying subject, as the auto-affective differentiation of self *as* self (Da-sein), horizonally and historically as in-the-world.

As difficult and as challenging as it may be, what Heidegger invites us to is anything but an academic exercise in self-indulgent intellectual theorizing. Fundamental ontology is not a predicative or representational thinking about being; rather it displaces the ordinary, metaphysical meanings of these terms, and in such a way that is intrinsically political and ethical, as a rigorous practice of careful interpretation, articulation, and disclosure.

## Technics constitute care

Are there clinical insights to be gleaned from Heidegger's reflections here? Yes, if we allow for a rethinking of the ethical and the political in ways that account for the possibility of the clinical from a psychoanalytic perspective—one concerned with interpretation of unconscious processes. Conceived as a practice of writing in its deconstructive sense—materially, technically—analytic care offers a response to the pathologies of the wish-world by refiguring (non-metaphysically) the relationship between mind and world, spirit and matter. This is where analysts have much to learn from the author of *Technics and Time* (1998, 2008, 2010a).

Stiegler's overall project attempts a rethinking of the relationship between the living and the non-living in order to consider the origins of the human in the interstices of this division and its dynamic instability. Building on, yet critically transforming, Heidegger and Derrida on the disavowal of finitude as constituting the philosophical tradition by means of the opposition between the empirical and the transcendental or between time and eternity, Stiegler recasts this debate in terms of the forgetting of the role of technical, material objects in the constitution of the symbolic. He argues that it is because of material, technical support for human memory that we form the capacity for symbolization by means of which we come to experience ourselves as capable of transcending the immediacy of the present "now." This capacity reflects not the presence of some unique and beatific soul but the complexity of the human nervous system as compared to that of the animal, which is similarly possessed of consciousness but not of a radically individuated sense of history capable of linking a self to a collective. Symbolization is anticipatory—it is open towards a future, and as such towards a past—in ways that integrate the three dimensions of temporality by producing symbolic connections that open the general field of history. What this means is that I can refer to *myself* only from out of a sense that I have an individual history in excess of the present moment, and in such a way that gives me a sense of a future toward which I am destined and over which I can exercise a degree of influence. What makes me capable of experiencing myself as a singular, individual subject is the fact that my conscious awareness repeatedly appropriates its past as its own in an ongoing effort to open onto a future figured by projects, interests, and desires. Human beings are human to the extent that they symbolize themselves in this particular way. Breakdowns in this capacity inaugurate processes of dehumanization and compulsions to act out violently.

Following Derrida, and against the classical tradition, Stiegler argues that in this way symbolic self-awareness is not an inherent biological or spiritual given but an effect of the possibility of organized material inscription (Derrida's "arche-writing"). That is, what is specific to human life (historical consciousness) emerges from out of a dynamic relationship between the living and the non-living—between the animal and inert matter. On the side of the living, evolutionary processes have evolved mnemic strategies that inscribe in the nervous system differences between the present and the past—what Stiegler, following Husserl (1991), calls "primary retentions" and "secondary retentions." Secondary retentions are remembrances of a past from which the present of the subjective sense of self immediately and constitutively distinguishes itself—memories in the everyday sense, in terms of the "vulgar" (Heidegger) distinction between past and present. Primary retentions are indicated by the moment-to-moment processes of memorization in the construction of symbolic meaning: In order to understand what it is that I am saying now, I must retain traces of what was said just a moment ago, and which efface themselves in the immediacy of the presence of meaning which is thereby produced as self-presence. In order to remember anything as a part of the past (secondary retention), I must immediately forget the difference between past and present, but in a way that makes any such distinction possible in the first place (primary retention). To remember the past "in" the present requires that I forget the separation-connection *between* past and present—that time as the differential constitution of past and present be forgotten so that an experience of memory as retentional storage becomes possible.

The forgetting of time as the difference between past and present, in the experience of the "now" in its absolute opposition to the past—that is, the construction of an opposition between the now of the present and the past as vulgar no-longer-now—depends upon the insistence or support of what Stiegler calls "tertiary retentions." This third form of memory is *matter*—the technical modification of material objects for the purpose of serving specifically human needs, and as these are generated, evolve and are handed down over generational time. For example, when I write down what I am thinking, so that I can come back to it later, this constitutes the possibility of my forgetting the difference between now and not-now, while at the same time forming a reliable basis for their distinction. Tertiary memories are located in external, material objects that support my sense of who I am as a psychological self, in that they can be discarded, forgotten and reappropriated as part of a material environment that appears as environment and not as (ideal) inner consciousness by means of this forgetfulness that *is* material inscription (again: arche-writing). Tertiary memories, as written traces of an intermittent moment of human experience that cannot be perpetually sustained but that must be materially historicized (i.e. recorded) both make possible and limit the emergence of the psychological experience of conscious understanding.

**112** Psychoanalysis and pharmacology

This is the sense in which, as Derrida elaborates, the trace—as the integration of biological life with inert matter that both generates and is generated by differance as "the becoming-time of space, the becoming-space of time," and that *haunts* life as the possibility of the *spirit* that orients us (or not) towards the future—is both and at the same time the condition of possibility and the condition of impossibility of the experience of consciousness as self-presence. What this means is that in order to have an experience of understanding we must immediately forget the passage of time in a hypostatization of the "now" in its difference from a memory kept in reserve. In order to remember anything in the psychological space of cognition, we depend upon the external, tertiary memory of modifiable, material support both to register and to erase temporal difference. Any awareness of an opposition between present and past—any subjective sense of being possessed of an individual history, as memory of the past opened upon the potential for a desirable future—depends upon the inscription of their forgotten connectedness. Material, technical inscription thus constitutes symbolic memory in the general economy of memory's erasure. This erasure is what makes possible both culture as collective spirit, and wish-world as generalized psychopathology. In *Taking Care of Youth and the Generations* (2010b), Stiegler writes:

> Given the wide variety of systemic environmental disorders that feed each other and are nothing more than the consequences of the destruction of caretaking systems, we face a situation that must be changed, and the consumer is the *central factor* in this system of autodestruction. The figure of the consumer, the pharmacological being who has been rendered structurally irresponsible and infantile (dependent), must be transcended, that is, taught once again to cultivate care and attention, through the structure of an industrial organization that must be reinvented.
>
> (p. 50; emphasis in original)

The figure of the consumer is the product of consumerism as a figure of care organized industrially—that is, in terms of the currently predominant form of the forgetting of the question of being. Stiegler translates Heidegger's account of Dasein as existential, auto-affective structure whereby time-temporalizes-itself into a critical appreciation of *consumption-consuming-itself* as the *organ*-ization (*Ge-stell*) of contemporary life. Speculative ("late") capitalism reflects consumption-consuming-itself as the articulation of ecstatic time that we are now inhabiting at a planetary level: auto-affection as auto-destruction. Where access to the experience of time is provided by a universal economy of industrially produced and commodified objects that actively destroys capacities for tertiary retention—practices of *writing* that facilitate *literacy*—attentiveness and desire are ruined at their very basis. As a result, there is no longer any politically available outside of this hyper-consumption, no resistance in a classical sense to the world in which we currently live. There are only local, individual—including *clinical*—strategies of more or less self-destruction, until a collective future can be gradually and eventually reconstituted.

## Maternal care—adoption and adaptation

Drawing together everything we have so far understood about the specificity of psychoanalysis as a clinical practice and about the ways in which it operates on the spectral limits that distinguish present, past and future while connecting them so as to form the very bases of memory, tradition and desire, we can now begin fully to consider questions that I have posed from the outset of the present text: To what extent is the analysand to be conceived of as a consumer of therapeutic care? What is the fate of interpretation as a modality of contemporary therapeutics organized as a marketplace of available techniques within which psychoanalysis is allocated a specific and receding place in an increasingly bureaucratized ("managed") economy of caretaking? If hyper-consumption functions today as the programmatic directive of culture as spirit—and in such a way that ruins this collective, spiritual dimension by atomizing individuality and by attacking all capacities for relatedness—should psychoanalysis be conceived of as participating in or as reacting against this program? Can the clinical become a site for reimagining the ethical and the political in ways that Heidegger first thought necessary? Answering these questions requires that we rethink—carefully, which is to say thoughtfully, without the sense that we already have the answers in advance—the nature and meaning of psychoanalytic technique in its capacity for modifying the psychic apparatus.

In *What Makes Life Worth Living: On Pharmacology*, Stiegler (2013) integrates Winnicott's thinking about transitional objects and transitional phenomena with the concerns that the three volumes of *Technics and Time* outline around the role of technical objects in the constitution of temporal, historical experience. Winnicott's account of the transitional object describes the foundational role that material things play in the generation of the child's psychic life. The essential task or technique of mothering in relation to this object consists in knowing not to challenge its status with regard to its having been discovered or created by the child herself (Winnicott 1971, p. 12). In this way the mother provides protection for the child's mind from the trauma of being forced prematurely into a decidable logic of either/or oppositions. The transitional object comes to embody this protection by functioning as both me and not-me in ways that promote integration of the emergent sense of self with environmental demand.

The prototype of the transitional object is the breast. According to Winnicott (1971), "the breast is created by the infant over and over again out of the infant's capacity to love or (one can say) out of need. A subjective phenomenon develops in the baby, which we call the mother's breast. The mother places the actual breast just where the infant is ready to create, and right at that moment" (p. 11). This describes how the generation of an experience of self is conditional upon need linked to repetition ("over and over again") and coordinated with the spatial proximity of the maternal body. The infant becomes a subject by repetitively creating something that is repetitively supplied to it by something that becomes an object through these coordinated acts of original repetition.

**114** Psychoanalysis and pharmacology

In a footnote to this passage, Winnicott distinguishes himself from the school of Melanie Klein by emphasizing that, for this very reason, the breast cannot be regarded merely as an object in the ordinary sense. Within the concept of the breast, Winnicott writes, "I include the whole *technique* of mothering. When it is said that the first object is the breast, the word 'breast' is used, I believe, to stand for *the technique of mothering as well as for the actual flesh*. It is not impossible for a mother to be a good enough mother (in my way of putting it) with a bottle for the actual feeding" (p. 11; emphases added). Winnicott here is not just making a typical pediatric value judgment that says the bottle-substitute is as adequate ("good enough") as the actual breast. He is making the more subtle point that the flesh-breast is no less technical than the bottle-breast, and that this is because maternal technique is essentially mechanical (repetitive).[1]

Given the general reception that governs his work in the analytic literature, it is difficult to appreciate just how at odds Winnicott is here with the tradition in psychoanalytic psychology called object relations. This tradition insists that the infant's relation to the mother is the essence of human being and is, as such, present at birth. For Winnicott in this passage, rather than being simply present (or simply absent, for that matter) at birth, object-relatedness is the effect of the identity of the maternal object and the technical (mechanical/processive) aspects of maternal practice. This identity is what is re-encountered/repeated by the child in the form of the transitional object (teddy bear, blanket, pillow, etc.) as something material that can be absolutely manipulated but that is also experienced as animated and mindful. When this emerges in the developing child's experience it is crucial that the mother not challenge or denigrate it by insisting on the priority of the ontic or of the real as actual—that she not impose a subject/object structure of opposition but instead provide for an experience in which the thing appears as having been both discovered and created. Doing so generates in the child the feeling of discovery which is met by a world waiting to be discovered—a world that is *there* (*Da*).

Stiegler (2013) expresses this same point by stating, "maternal knowledge is *knowledge of that which, in the transitional object, consists, though it does not exist*, and which gives to the child placed under this protection the feeling that 'life is worth living'" (p. 2; emphasis in original). In that it consists without existing, the transitional object stands in excess of its material being. This excess—the particular form the transitional object takes in the child's economy of objects with which it is presented and in which it invests—is a symbolic excess that allows the object to be individually unique and special, to stand out amongst objects as something more than a mere object, as both living and non-living due to an investment that is both libidinal and in excess of ordinary libidinal investment. For Winnicott, ordinary libidinal investments are the effect, not the cause, of transitional phenomena. Stiegler sees in this reversal an opportunity to graft the Heideggerian distinction between the ontic and the ontological onto the psychoanalytic domain. In that it functions both as a material and as an ideal presence, the transitional object supports the integration of these two (ontic and ontological) planes on which human life is played out: "*things* can constitute a *world* only insofar as they irreducibly proceed from the transitional character of the object" (p. 3; emphases in original).

To the extent that she does not defensively challenge but is capable of creatively encouraging the child's experience of transitional phenomena, the mother—like the transitional object itself—functions as a figure of tertiary retention: not as object as autonomous, subjective, living being but as the material inscription of memory as an organization of reality as active dependence. The mother's ability to anticipate the child's needs, and to be there "over and over again" at just the right (but never the actual real) moment in order to provide "at the beginning…an almost 100 per cent adaptation" (Winnicott 1971, p. 11) makes her a form of external support for the child's evolving memory-apparatus. This evolution is not just that of a cognitive faculty; it concerns the cultivation of desire, creativity and interest in the world (the "not-me"). This is why Winnicott, in the passage quoted above, equates love with need: not because the baby needs love, but because the mother's mechanical, repetitive response to the baby's need is what first opens up in the baby the capacity to care by introducing "an *almost* 100 per cent adaptation"—by introducing difference at the origin.

What this means is that the mother is not primarily what the baby relates "to" but what constitutes the possibility of the baby's related*ness*. The experience of the mother as object of active dependence is not that to which the infant, in its helplessness, stands under and opposed (as subjected)—it is that that *through* which the infant learns to relate *to itself* in the element of unspoken maternal caregiving. Maternal knowledge is not knowledge in the form of conscious understanding communicated to the child, but knowledge as indistinguishable from practical procedures of caregiving that, eventually mediated by the child's relationship to the transitional object, make the experience of conscious knowledge or careful understanding possible in the first place. This is what it means to say that there is no understanding without inscription, no inside without outside. The constitution of reflective interiority or psychic space begins here with a putting-in-reserve towards an outside that is only constituted as outside in a gesture that dynamically *transitions* back and forth between the me and the not-me. There is no mother or child in the absence of material objects that encourage and facilitate their differentiation into a system of mutually effected care. This is not, however, an Oedipal triangle of relations between subjects and objects in any ordinary sense: the uncanny (living/non-living) technical-mothering-thing exists only *as* its relation to the child as auto-affective, individuating process by means of the material (tertiary) object (breast, blanket, bear) that is not objectively real but dynamically transitional (between me and not-me). Mother and child are in this way brought into a system of mutual adoption, relating to one another though the intermediary of the transitional object that both contingently precedes and that formally emerges as singular from out of their circuit of reciprocal fascination.

Maternal technique thus does not consist merely in the satisfaction of biological need, nor does it belong solely to the primary caretaker but to all adults charged with cultivating children's well-being. Central among such techniques is that of playing which, of course, was always at the heart of Winnicott's investigations. According to Stiegler (2010b), "*To play* with a child is to take care of the child, opening

**116** Psychoanalysis and pharmacology

the paths by which transitional spaces are created, paths that stimulate the origins of art, culture, and ultimately everything that forms the symbolic order" (p. 14; emphasis in original). Stiegler follows Winnicott here virtually word for word, but what he emphasizes is that playing is not a purely spontaneous, free activity that can be naively opposed to technical, disciplinary procedures of parenting. Playing constitutes rather a technique for creating transitional space and for encouraging relational engagement beyond the auto-destructive demands of the wish-world: "a transitional space is first and foremost a *system* of caring" (p. 15; emphasis added).

For Freud, the encounter with the outside world is an imposition on the child's drives, curbing the pleasure principle by imposing the principle of reality. Freud is thus generally constrained to portray civilized culture as irreducibly repressive. Winnicott understands the relationship between the individual and the social as intrinsically creative: the outside world—which is not merely outside in the sense of a given opposition, but originally not-me as differentially other—cannot just demand that the child repress her desires; it must invite the child to connect her desire up to the world at large, to invest care: "the mother must *bring* the child to *adopt*—or not—its *transitional situation*, that is its *pharmacological situation*, on the basis of which the child will be *able* to attain, or not, the feeling that life is worth living" (Stiegler 2013, p. 3; emphases in original). A healthy life is one in which we are able to capitalize on our childhood capacity to play by investing in shared, cultural experience. Maturity consists not in giving up on our capacity to play in order to submit to the exigencies of work in the service of adaptation and survival, but in becoming capable of expanding our access to transitional phenomena in ways that cover and that adopt the socio-cultural field at large.

Where Freud thinks about renunciation, Winnicott thinks in terms of integration. Renunciation, which amounts ultimately to a renunciation of creative care, can only lead to conditions that Stiegler has called *symbolic misery* according to which, in the absence of any capacity to articulate symbolically their being as care, human beings find nothing to connect themselves up to in the world, having been deprived of an experience of world *as* world (i.e. as the site of transitional *phenomena*). Under such conditions, administrative systems replace institutional traditions in order to enforce adaptation to a world that we increasingly cannot adopt as our own and in relation to which we feel little sense of belonging. Enforced adaptation inevitably leads not only to disillusionment but to the discovery of euphoria in unchannelled destructiveness. What Heidegger had called care is the alternative basis on which we create the possibility of attachment and of caretaking *systems* that form the infrastructure of all social and familial existence: "care is what makes possible a *process of adoption*—of the child by its mother, and of the transitional object by the mother-child pair, within which the 'mother' is the educator through which is created what Bowlby described as the relation of attachment…care is a process of adoption, and … *precisely not adaptation*. Adaptation is the source of the bad relation to the transitional object, according to Winnicott" (Stiegler 2013, p. 134, n.1; emphases in original). Adoption involves the integration of self and environment on a plane of temporal consistency as openness to (future) possibility. Adaptation involves splitting apart self and environment through submission to existence as the merely actual real. Transitional phenomena are to be located at the juncture of these two forms of relatedness, or as the relation between relation and non-relation.

For Winnicott, this juncture marks the transitional or differantial coordination of creativity and addiction: "At this point my subject widens out into that of play, and of artistic creativity and appreciation, and of religious feeling, and of dreaming, and also of fetishism, lying and stealing, the origin and loss of affectionate feeling, drug addiction, the talisman of obsessional rituals, etc." (Winnicott 1971, p. 5). This is also the point at which Winnicott begins to speak a spectral vocabulary in relation to the developmental trajectory of the transitional object: "Its fate is to be gradually allowed to be decathected, so that in the course of years it becomes not so much forgotten as *relegated to limbo*" (ibid.; emphasis added). Beyond the metaphysical opposition of memory and forgetfulness, the transitional object comes to occupy a temporal space between past and present, a background that is neither present nor absent—a state of "limbo" that generally escapes reflection but that makes possible everyday libidinal investments, projects and desires. As an effort to cultivate such investments, the analytic relationship constitutes a caretaking system that issues from the maintenance of its technical frame.

However, the reference to fetishism, to lying and stealing, to drug addiction and obsession as continuous with rather than as opposed to playing, creativity and dreaming is indicative of what is at stake in a clinic that aspires to be something more than yet another form of authoritarian engagement. Such an aspiration is what has set the psychoanalytic clinic apart since Freud's attempts rigorously to distance himself from procedures of suggestion and hypnosis. Psychoanalysis conceived as clinical play must be more than a subdivision of mental health practices that promote adaptation to existing conditions of symbolic misery. The pervasive ideology of mental health today—which permeates everything from the pharmaceutical industry to daily television programming—functions fetishistically, addictively. Historically and traditionally, psychoanalysis has at once turned itself toward and distinguished itself from these trends; it will always remain fundamentally exposed to appropriations that undermine its more radical intentions and possibilities. Intrinsic to the Derridean logic of the *pharmakon* is the understanding that efforts to resist and to dismantle control will always resemble and threaten to devolve into procedures of control. It is precisely for this reason, and because its clinic functions unlike any other as a privileged site of transitional phenomena, that psychoanalysis today must define itself in opposition to the currently prevailing tendencies—but not the *spirit*—of the mental health industry, by embracing techniques of adoption rather than of adaptation.

## Possibility

In her polemic, *Why Psychoanalysis?* (2001), Elisabeth Roudinesco writes:

> All the sociological studies … show that the tendency of [our] depressive society is to destroy the essence of human resistance. Between the fear of disorder and the valorization of a competitiveness based only on material

## 118 Psychoanalysis and pharmacology

success, there are many subjects who prefer to give themselves over willingly to chemical substances rather than speak of their private sufferings. The power of medicines of the mind is thus the symptom of a modernity tending toward the abolition not only of the desire for liberty but also of the very idea of confronting that experience. Silence is therefore preferable to language, which is a source of distress and shame.

(p. 18)

Whether or not it is actually the case that "all the sociological studies" indicate a tendency to destroy resistance and to enforce narcotic apathy, the position of psychoanalysis within the mental health professions today is indicative of major reversals in cultural values over a historically brief period of time. These reversals in no way reflect popular demand for therapeutic intervention but are instead programmed by conditions imposed by the global marketplace. Roudinesco's romanticism is admirable, but ultimately misguided. What Stiegler allows us to appreciate is that psychoanalysis is not a humanistic alternative to instrumental forms of clinical intervention, that it is *no less pharmacological* than market-based therapeutic strategies (drugs, CBT, ECT, etc.), though it intrinsically tends more toward auto-affective, individuating-relational adoption than toward further auto-destructive investment in administration and behavioral management. What Stiegler gives clinicians to consider is that it is neither as a paternal authority figure nor as an empathic maternal object but as technical care-giver that the analyst is capable of cultivating difference, transformation and change.[2] As a practitioner of neutrality and of interpretation in the context of a stable, open frame, and in response to the patient's efforts at free association, the analyst serves as a function of the transitional caretaking environment itself, not as an administrator of therapeutic technique. Unlike cognitive and behavioral approaches, for which technique constitutes no more than a mode of communicating conscious disciplinary knowledge, analytic technique cannot be distinguished from the analyst himself or herself as neutral interpreter of transitional, transferential relation.

Roudinesco is nevertheless certainly correct in diagnosing a crisis of psychoanalysis that reflects wider social crises—crises that should make psychoanalysis appear more relevant now than ever. As any clinician can readily attest to, patients who present themselves for analysis today frequently protest that if the analyst "really cared" he would not charge a fee for his time, that sessions would go on for extended periods, that all sorts of interpersonal interactions would be permitted and not regarded as transgressions of the analytic frame. Such are the demands of the contemporary wish-world: for an experience of the other as an object of consumption; for relationality to be reduced to simple variations on humanistic intersubjectivity; to divert time and money away from practices that promote intimate and complex relational connectedness; avoidance of any experience of time as play which cannot be calculated or programmed according to logics of investment and return. The crises that the future of the psychoanalytic clinic is inevitably confronted with today can be approached either as cause for mourning and resignation or as opportunities for affirmation and renewal. Deconstruction provides us with the resources necessary for choosing the latter in the face of so much appalling carelessness.

## Notes

1  Bass (2006) references a similar instance from another paper of the same period where Winnicott discusses "the mother's technique" (1954, p. 263), though he regards this as a mere "flash" (p. 114). What Bass calls "the 'technological' mother of primary narcissism" is precisely what is at issue in Stiegler's approach to a more general critical thinking of technics and care in the context of culture and of what he calls "industrial politics." This is why, I believe, Winnicott has become increasingly central to Stiegler's project. The concepts of the transitional object and of transitional phenomena provide a possible starting point for a rigorously psychoanalytic thinking about the relationship between mind and technical articulation. As I outlined in Chapter 2, this effort has tremendous practical consequences for thinking the clinical effectiveness of the psychoanalytic frame.
2  As indicated in my previous note above, there is considerable overlap on this point between Stiegler's orientation and Bass who wishes to situate himself exclusively in terms of the psychoanalytic clinic. However, Stiegler is more conventionally materialist in his approach, while Bass naturally insists on the clinic as the site of a primarily psychological practice. Where Bass (2006, p. 45; pp. 135–136) seems to accuse Winnicott of remaining too metaphysical in his thinking of transitional *phenomena* empirically as transitional *objects*, Stiegler affirms the category of the object in order to underscore the *transitional* character of modifiable, material inscription as tertiary *memorization*. Both would agree that transitional objects embody or inscribe differantial space-time. Since neither of these orientations is intended to be absolute, it is not a question here of privileging either one or the other, but of integrating these projects together in a "double affirmation" that would link clinical practice to critical, political interventions today, beyond the mediation of a traditional conceptual attitude.

## References

Bass, A. (2006). *Interpretation and Difference: The Strangeness of Care*. Stanford, CA: Stanford University Press.

Beardsworth, R. (1995). "From a Genealogy of Matter to a Politics of Memory: Stiegler's Thinking of Technics." *Tekhnema: Journal of Philosophy and Technology*, 2: 85–115.

Curtis, A. Dir. (2002). *Century of the Self*.

Derrida, J. (1981). *Dissemination*. Trans. B. Johnson. Chicago, IL: University of Chicago Press.

Freud, S. (1930). *Civilization and Its Discontents*. S.E. 21: pp. 57–146.

Grosskurth, P. (1977). *Melanie Klein: Her World and Her Work*. Northvale, NJ: Jason Aronson.

Heidegger, M. (1966). *Discourse on Thinking*. Trans. J. Anderson and E. Freund. New York: Harper and Row.

Heidegger, M. (1977). *The Question Concerning Technology and other essays*. Trans. W. Lovitt. New York: Harper Torchbooks.

Heidegger, M. (1990). *Kant and the Problem of Metaphysics*. Trans. R. Taft. Bloomington, IN: Indiana University Press.

Heidegger, M. (1996). *Being and Time*. Trans. J. Stambaugh. Albany, NY: SUNY Press.

Husserl, E. (1991). *On the Phenomenology of the Internal Consciousness of Time: 1893–1917*. Trans. J. Barnett Brough. Boston, MA: Kluwer Academic Publisher.

**120** Psychoanalysis and pharmacology

Kierkegaard, S. (1962). *The Present Age: On the Death of Rebellion.* Trans. A. Dru. New York: Harper Perennial.

Kierkegaard, S. (1980). *The Sickness Unto Death.* Ed. and Trans. H.V. Hong and E. H. Hong. Princeton, NJ: Princeton University Press.

Loewald, H. (1988). *Sublimation: An Essay in Theoretical Psychoanalysis.* New Haven, CT: Yale University Press.

Marcuse, H. (2002). *One-Dimensional Man.* Boston, MA: Beacon Press, 1964.

Roudinesco, E. (2001). *Why Psychoanalysis?* Trans. Rachel Bowlby. New York: Columbia University Press.

Stiegler, B. (1998). *Technics and Time, Volume 1: The Fault of Epimetheus.* Trans. R. Beardsworth and G. Collins. Stanford, CA: Stanford University Press.

Stiegler, B. (2008). *Technics and Time, Volume 2: Disorientation.* Trans. S. Barker. Stanford, CA: Stanford University Press.

Stiegler, B. (2010a). *Technics and Time, Volume 3: Cinematic Time and the Question of Malaise.* Trans. S. Barker. Stanford, CA: Stanford University Press.

Stiegler, B. (2010b). *Taking Care of Youth and the Generations.* Trans. S. Barker. Stanford, CA: Stanford University Press.

Stiegler, B. (2013). *What Makes Life Worth Living: On Pharmacology.* Trans. D. Ross. Malden, MA: Polity Press.

Winnicott, D.W. (1954). "The Depressive Position in Normal Emotional Development." In: *Through Pediatrics to Psychoanalysis* (1975). New York: Basic Books.

Winnicott, D.W. (1971). *Playing and Reality.* New York: Routledge.

# POSTSCRIPT

## The trauma of the clinic of the telepathic machine

While I was completing work on this manuscript, a patient brought to her analysis the following dream. She prefaced her telling of the dream by saying that she had intended not to tell me about it—not because of any desire to conceal from me its contents, but because the dream itself had been so upsetting that she did not want to repeat the experience by remembering it.

In the first part of the dream she is driving a car in her hometown, in the foreign country of her origin. She realizes that she is thirty minutes late to one of our appointments, and that I must be waiting for her, alone, not knowing what is happening. She has the thought to call me on her cellular phone, but she is overwhelmed by the sense that she has wasted my time, and that as a result she has ruined our relationship. She feels such an overwhelming sense of loss that it is almost as if she has killed me and that I am dead.

Suddenly she and I are present together in her childhood home, in her bedroom. I am on the phone speaking an unrecognizable language that makes no sense, a language that bears no resemblance to any recognizable or even possible human language. She cannot understand what I am saying, but it makes her smile. She understands that her high school boyfriend—her first love, who had figured prominently in the early stages of the analysis—is outside the bedroom window and is about to peer inside. She does not want him to see us together, and she says to me, "Duck!"

The old boyfriend does look in the window and sees that she is holding several of her own drawings in her hand. Something about his eyes indicates that he wants to see the drawings up close. This makes her angry and anxious. She does not want him to see the drawings because they contain some sort of message about her intensely positive feelings towards me. Again she instructs me to "duck!" At this point, she says, she woke up anxious and wanting to forget about the dream entirely, but it has nevertheless stayed with her.

**122** Postscript

We are both silent. Eventually I repeat, "duck." Several seconds of silence pass between us until she intones, "Hmm…"

More silence passes between us. She says, "I hadn't thought of that…" Then, "I see what you mean…"

After another brief silence she says that she also understands how, to an outside observer, like her old boyfriend looking in through the window, this intervention would have appeared meaningless and would have made no sense. Its meaningfulness depends upon the history of the radically intimate relationship that we have privately cultivated together.

Over the past few months the patient had intermittently elaborated a fantasy of our going together to see the ducks at a pond in the park near my office. On a few occasions she had even gone there by herself and thought of what it would be like to be there with me. While discussing this fantasy with her, at one point I had slipped and made reference to her fantasy that we were going to *feed* the ducks together. She quickly responded that she had said nothing about *feeding* the ducks, that her fantasy was just about going to see them with me, and that feeding them had been my own supplementary elaboration. She then said she imagined that feeding the ducks was something I had done as a child with my mother.

The patient had been in analysis long enough to recognize this as a transferential fantasy. What she could not have known was that she was absolutely correct: my mother had on several occasions taken me to feed the ducks at a local pond when I was a child. This was a memory I had not had access to in decades, and in the moment of its sudden and unexpected reappearance it seemed to symbolize my relationship with my mother throughout my childhood. Although my mother had died some years previously (a fact of which the patient had been made aware), in my experience I had mourned her loss and had integrated it into my sense of myself and of the course of my life. But when the patient made this comment about her fantasy—which was also my memory—the pain of losing a parent suddenly became so overwhelmingly intense that it was as if I were registering the loss all over again, as if for the first time. The patient was on the couch and could not see the grimace of pain on my face, and I managed just barely to successfully suppress a cry of emotion. It felt as if she had reached into my mind and retrieved an important yet forgotten memory for me.

In the session where she was now reporting the dream about our being together in her childhood bedroom, in relation to which I had made the intervention "duck," she says that she thinks the dream is about how deeply connected to me she feels, and how this sometimes feels threatened by the world outside my office—a world that could cause her to lose me forever. I found it extremely difficult to prompt her for more associations to the material.

In my own associations to the dream I found myself preoccupied with her having twice mentioned the presence of the telephone. I thought of the passage from Freud's "Recommendations to Physicians" on the unconscious as a telephone, in relation to Derrida's writings on telepathy, and about which I had published a paper in the course of the previous year (an early version of what appears in the present text as Chapter 3, and which I was at the time reworking for the purpose of publishing it as part of this volume). I recalled that when she had "retrieved" my childhood memory for me, I'd had the counter-transferential impulse in that moment to tell her about the paper that I had written, to explain to her that Freud had written about experiences like the one that had just occurred between us, and that a famous French philosopher had also drawn attention to instances like the one we were presently involved in. This would only have served to suppress my own pain by intellectualizing the analytic process, so I had kept quiet.

Now, however, I could not stop thinking about the significance of the telephone in the patient's dream. About how the dream was indeed a representation of the depth of our intimate clinical connection. About how in the dream I was speaking a nonsensical language that was still more meaningful than any phonetic communication. About how her pictographic drawings contained messages about me as if written in a language that functioned otherwise than as a representation of speech. And about how from a certain perspective this would describe a form of writing as telepathic connection prior to language as speech, one that can only appear aleatory and that makes no sense when tended to directly but that makes experiences like sense and connection and intimacy possible.

I wanted to tell the patient all of this, and to tell her about my writing, which could only have been a gesture of narcissistic imposition. I had been suppressing the impulse to do this for some time, perhaps ever since she had first indicated to me that she had learned that my mother had died, or at least ever since my own analyst had subsequently died, something the patient did not know about. I realized that I had been wanting to tell all of my patients about all of this, about myself and about my own experience, to turn their analyses into my analysis. I had resisted doing so because my training had allowed me to grasp, without having consciously had to articulate it theoretically, just how destructive such a violation of the clinical frame this would have been.

In this moment, however, with this particular patient, according to the immense amount of emotional pain that we were both individually containing and that we were silently attracting each other towards as a way of communicating with one another—and for me against the background of the writing I was working on which gave me reason to hope in the midst of so much loss—the question as to who was in analysis with whom disclosed not a narcissistic struggle over who was in control of the transference, but a dimension of clinical intimacy in which formal distinctions between subjects and objects are factically irrelevant. It was as if the patient had quite rigorously, if unconsciously and without understanding, "read" what I had written—she had "seen" what "I mean"—without any conscious awareness of having done so, or by means of a form of literacy that consciousness cannot account for or make sense of. This was an uncanny instance in which the patient's dream was the fulfillment of the analyst's unconscious wish.

I imagine that occurrences such as this are more frequent than analysts are ready to admit, and that such instances register what had led someone as deeply

**124** Postscript

committed to scientific rationalism as Freud to take an abiding interest in the occult topic of telepathy.

In the series of interviews with Elisabeth Roudinesco to which I referred in the preface, Derrida was invited to comment on the topic of freedom, a concept that he claimed rarely to have made use of. The invitation occurs in the context of a larger question about the difference between science and scientism—between an authentically open spirit of scientific investigation, to which deconstruction would belong, and a religiously governed version of scientific discourse that must exclude in principle anything like deconstruction or psychoanalysis.

Derrida's response was to situate this difference in the context of a more general reflection on the nature of the machine. Scientism relies upon the fetishization of machines, of grand technological frameworks that operate machines in order to produce experiences of satisfaction in having arrived smoothly and efficiently at the production of certifiable results. Results are what can be bought and sold in the marketplace of behavioral research, which is supported today by industries of marketing and advertising. The production of results is not science, it is what remains when the creativity of the scientific spirit has been reduced to the formalism of administrative procedure. This always involves an image of thought reduced to calculation, to the exclusion of any instance of the unexpected or of the unpredictable. In the intellectual history of the West, deconstruction is a form of philosophy as resistance that necessarily emerges at those moments when the spirit of creative scientific endeavor is coopted by regional, narrow-minded interests concerned primarily with proof, profit and productivity.

Critics of Derrida and of other Continental philosophers of his generation who had affirmed their debt to Nietzsche and to Heidegger often make much of these authors' alleged "anti-humanism." This is not a derogatory term invented by those critics, although that is often how it is used, as synonymous with an anti-democratic orientation. It is a label that Derrida rejected, regarding anti-humanism as yet another version of humanism or of metaphysics (1982, pp. 118–119). In his discussion of scientism, however, the anti-humanist tendencies of deconstruction clearly emerge. This has to do with a refusal to identify with an image of the human to the detriment of a care for the machine, as a way of concealing or demeaning the machinic dimensions of human life or of life as such. Derrida admits that, much like the uncritical scientism he deplores, he shares a fascination with the machine and with the complexity of machines, a fascination that he says is "necessary." Why necessary? "In my opinion, the most 'free' thought is the one that is constantly coming to terms with the effects of the machine" (Derrida & Roudinesco 2004, p. 48). Which is why, he says, he keeps his distance from the word "freedom." What was Derrida getting at here?

Humanism will always valorize the human over and above the machine, as the living embodiment of spontaneity and freedom, the opposite of which would be the dead machine—lifeless, inorganic, repetitive and closed in on itself. This is the unthought and groundless metaphysical hierarchy that Derrida had identified from his earliest texts on in the prioritization of speech over writing. As a metaphysical project humanism is not the defense of human dignity, rather it is the idealization of such dignity over and above life itself which is shot through at every level with machines and programs, as every discourse of the contemporary life sciences teaches us. Equating the question of the role of the machine in the processes of life with a naive determinism lacking in openness and complexity, humanism is the rejection of any association of the human with the machine, with the technical, with that which can be programmed and controlled. Where the fact that human beings can be programmed and controlled is disavowed, industries of programming and control take root and begin to operate, often rather smoothly and efficiently. As Herbert Marcuse once famously wrote, "A comfortable, smooth, reasonable, democratic unfreedom prevails in advanced industrial civilization, a token of technical progress" (2002, p. 3). Deconstruction shares this perception, whereas its strategy is not to demonize technical progress but to ask instead about the self-understanding of the being that finds itself in the midst of such a historical, global crisis. What can sound foreboding when presented under the sign of an "anti-humanist" orientation is in fact an effort not to be so quick in confidently providing definitions of what the human consists in and of what can stand in opposition to it.

The wholesale rejection of the analogy between mind and machine in contemporary psychoanalysis is the source of a tremendous amount of pride among clinicians. An emphasis on the influence of the early environment over the productions of fantasy; the valorization of object relations and the abandonment of the concept of the drive; the transference having replaced the dream as the royal road to the unconscious; the retreat of the concept of the unconscious and the advance of a theory of the self—all of these developments are driven by a belief that progress in psychoanalysis requires distancing ourselves from Freud's approach to the psyche as apparatus, and by means of a resurgent investment in centered models of humanist subjectivity. For Derrida, who seems unaware of this trajectory in the history of psychoanalysis, this would constitute a betrayal by means of which what is most original in Freud's thinking might ultimately be lost:

> But the very aim, and I do say the *aim*, of the psychoanalytic revolution is the only one not to rest, not to seek refuge, in principle, in what I call a theological or humanist alibi. That is why it can appear terrifying, terribly cruel, pitiless. Even to psychoanalysts, even to those who, on both sides of the couch, more or less pretend to put their trust in psychoanalysis.
>
> (2004, p. 173; emphasis in original)

The epidemic regression to Cartesianism in the contemporary psychoanalytic literature indicates that there is less pretending than one might hope, and that even analysts themselves trust little in psychoanalysis these days without having to modify it, perhaps for the purpose of commodifying it.

At the same time, it is this very question of modification and of modifiability that is at the heart of Derrida's appeal to the creativity of the machine metaphor, which

**126** Postscript

reveals itself to be more than a mere metaphor. Neither humanism (as an effort uncritically to refuse this metaphor and its rich cultural history) nor scientism (as an effort uncritically to insist on this metaphor, so as to deny not only its historicity but its metaphoricity as well) are capable of appreciating this resource. At its worst this failure indicates a certain unexpected complicity, a place where humanism and scientism coincide, amplifying each others' tendencies toward fundamentalism. In contrast to this dangerous complicity, what deconstruction locates is the fact that, "in the machine there is an excess in relation to the machine itself: at once the effect of a machination and something that eludes machinelike calculation" (p. 49). Derrida identifies this excess with that term which, in virtually the same breath, he claims never to speak of: "freedom is an excess of play in the machine" (p. 48). Asked about this freedom at play within the psychic apparatus as demonstrated by the experience of affective intensity, he responded:

> The difficulty, it seems to me, is to take into account the possibility of this extreme, extended, and extendable mechanization, and to forget that there is a point where calculation reaches its limit: play, the possibility of play within calculating machines. And what you call affect, that is, the relation of the living being to the other—the relation to oneself as a relation to another—this affect remains, by definition, incalculable, something foreign to all machines [...] something that resists analysis and thus always remains to be analyzed. It is no doubt through this irreducibility of affect, that is, of the other and the relation to the other, that what we still call freedom or the unconscious should be reintroduced, but without falling into a reactionary ideology.
>
> (p. 58)

What this indicates is that the Freudian unconscious should not be understood as what programs and determines all conscious thought and behavior in advance. The unconscious is rather that very excess of freedom and play that makes something like the psyche at all possible within the context of the organic machine, which is to say in the context of the history of life as trace. This excess would be constitutive of the human yet in no way limited to it. Such excess would also be constitutive of psychoanalysis yet in no way limited to it, because it is what makes the psychic apparatus modifiable with respect to a certain critical or interpretive rigor. Derrida understood that, for Freud, the psyche is interpretively, therapeutically modifiable precisely *because* it constitutes an apparatus and *not* an egological soul or self. The unconscious is this excess of play intrinsic to the psychic machine, which is what distinguishes the Freudian unconscious from the subconscious of the cognitivists, both before and after Freud.

The Freudian concept of the psychic apparatus is neither reductive nor crudely mechanistic. To the contrary, as a concept—which is to say, as a symbol—it is deeply playful and paradoxical. "Whatever may be thought of the continuities and ruptures to come," Derrida wrote of the mystic writing pad in 1966, "this hypothesis is remarkable as soon as it is considered as a metaphorical model and not as a neurological description" (1978, p. 200). What is *remarkable*—what insistently, repeatedly leaves a mark, a trace that can be discerned if only one remembers how to look for it—is the fact that this hypothesis that minds and machines are irreducibly co-implicated, is not dialectizable or recuperable within the struggle between those who would defend humanity against a technological encroachment and those who would see in technology a messianic saving power. Freud's *Seeleapparat* is an invitation to another framework, another reading. Read together, deconstruction and psychoanalysis point us out of this impasse in which the subjective and the objective, mind and matter, the organic and the inorganic can only appear opposed to one another and in ways that can only authorize increasingly destructive strategies of administration and control. As I have attempted to outline, such a reading would provide us with the possibility for conceiving of other forms of reading and of writing that would account for and that would cultivate the kind of "resonance" upon which a clinic of interpretation is predicated. This is an experience that the entire history of metaphysics—from its religious to its secular versions, and as these have been handed down everywhere by priests of one sort or another—has attempted to control because of its traumatically disruptive and therefore potentially revolutionary power.

The rejection of the technological model of the psychic apparatus in psychoanalysis has often proceeded by way of embracing another technological model, one that does a great deal more to conceal its technicity: the model of the mind as mirror. The mirror is a technology undecidably inscribed between narcissism and self-reflection. In psychoanalysis the mirror always appears bound to the figure of the mother, as a way of describing what both separates and connects, whether this is conceived either as a barrier that distorts and that bars the subject from the other (as for Lacan) or as precisely what conjoins self and other in the element of empathy and mutual understanding (as for Winnicott and Kohut). The intersection of deconstruction and psychoanalysis is situated in excess of this analogy of the mirror. The trace that is registered in the persistence of this analogy that insistently links mind and technical artifact, even when it is precisely this analogy that is being refused, is the trace of the meaning of the possibility of metaphor or of symbolization. This trace persists in the form of a question because it always remains suspended between the material and the ideal, or between the practical and the theoretical, like the disciplines of deconstruction and psychoanalysis themselves.

In an essential text in the history of deconstruction, Rodolphe Gasché (1986) provided an account of the Derridean trace in terms of the *tain* of the mirror—the black underside of the mirror's reflective surface, the side that is not seen, that does not reflect the subject back to itself but that makes reflection functionally possible. Gasché demonstrated that the philosophical and scientific import of deconstruction was to have challenged the fetishization of the mirror that insists within—if not that which defines—the tradition of the West, which sees itself everywhere reflected in the world, to the extent that this becomes increasingly, globally true at every turn. The Derridean trace is not a mirror, it does not reflect and one does not stand before it passively and receive an image of oneself as when one sees in nature

**128** Postscript

a reflection of "man" or in the world a reflection of Europe or of America. As an inscrutable underside that dissimulates itself in order to make immediate reflection both materially and psychologically possible, the trace invites an act of *reading*. With regard to the status of the Western tradition today, this reading is an effort to decipher a past that was never present, that was never properly *mine* nor *ours* but that is possessed of the means through which we become ourselves in repeating acts of appropriation, such as reading and writing, which are technical and unnatural, at least according to a metaphysical position that continues to oppose the natural and the technical, the historical and the ideal.

The capacity for this reading, which is at once a practice of individuation—a practice of "the most radical individuation"—is everywhere exposed to the possibility of its being destroyed, as the trace is defined by its fundamental exposure to erasure, in that it exists *as* erased in becoming, beyond the opposition of presence and absence. What this means is that the past that we share—and to the extent that this past was never our own in a possessively individual sense, rather a past that was always already there in the form of a history and a tradition waiting to be taken up and renewed by each of us, together—is an excess of freedom, an excess that does not finally liberate but that *binds*, in the double sense of both bringing us together and constituting a problem. Wherever we are capable of modifying ourselves (as in philosophy, beyond its having been reduced to a university discourse), and wherever we are similarly capable of modifying one another (as in psychoanalysis, beyond its having been reduced to a practice of mental health counseling) we discover the traces of that which both separates and connects us in this generalized and traumatic vulnerability, this resonating circuit of ecstatic time that is the persistent and haunting *Hilflosigkeit* originally thematized by Freud.

## References

Derrida, J. (1978). "Freud and the Scene of Writing." In: *Writing and Difference*. Trans. A. Bass. Chicago, IL: University of Chicago Press. Pp. 196–231.

Derrida, J. (1982). "The Ends of Man." In: *Margins—of Philosophy*. Trans. A. Bass. Chicago, IL: University of Chicago Press. Pp. 109–136.

Derrida, J., & Roudinesco, E. (2004). *For What Tomorrow…* Trans J. Fort. Stanford, CA: Stanford University Press.

Gasché, R. (1986). *The Tain of the Mirror*. Cambridge, MA: Harvard University Press.

Marcuse, H. (2002). *One-Dimensional Man*. Boston, MA: Beacon Press. 1964.

# INDEX

absence 18, 29, 35, 40, 43–45, 47, 49, 55–57, 60–61, 63, 74, 77–78, 85, 91, 97, 109, 115–116, 128
activity 20, 22, 24, 26, 41, 48–49, 51–53, 60, 63, 65, 74–75, 78, 81–82, 115
adaptation 87, 113, 115–117
addiction 43–44, 100, 104, 106–109, 117; and addictogenic 43
administration 75, 106, 118, 127
adoption 16, 113, 115–118
aesthetic 7, 50, 97
agency 14, 20, 97
American Psychiatric Association 2
analytic frame 6, 37–40, 44, 47, 53–54, 58, 61, 82, 85–86, 91, 118, 119n1; clinical frame 6–7, 35, 38–41, 44–47, 53, 56, 58–60, 64, 66–67, 67n1–n2, 80, 90–91, 123; psychoanalytic frame 46, 53–54, 60; and technical frame 103, 117
analytic third 55
anti-deconstructive 3
anti-humanism *see* humanism
anxiety 42, 51, 62–63, 79–80, 83, 86, 101, 107
apparatus 5, 7, 88, 100, 125–126; memory-apparatus 115; mind-brain apparatus 88; psychic apparatus 66, 80, 113, 126–127; and psychical apparatus 78
archive 66
Aristotle 72, 106
articulation 15, 66, 75, 77, 97, 100, 108, 110, 112
artistic production 7, 48
attachment 116

attunement 88
authoritarian *see* authoritarianism
authoritarianism 2–3, 5, 40, 76, 84, 89, 103, 105, 117
auto-affection 24–25, 46, 49, 51, 66, 78, 81–82, 89, 99, 110, 112, 115, 118
auto-destructive 116, 118
autonomy 43, 76, 97, 100, 102, 105

Bass, Alan 67n1, 119n1–n2
Beardsworth, Richard 106
Bernays, Edward 97
bi-temporality *see* temporality
bind 29, 54, 64, 81, 85, 96, 106, 128
Bion, Wilfred 47, 87, 92n3
Birksted-Breen, Dana 8, 71, 83–91, 92n3, 93n4
Bleger, José 7, 39, 52–64, 68n5–n6; and "Psycho-Analysis of the Psycho-Analytic Frame" 7, 53
Bollas, Christopher 7, 81–83, 91n1–92n1
Bourdieu, Pierre 2
Bowlby, John 116
breast 113–115 *see also* mother-infant matrix
Breton, André 4

care 41, 89–90, 98, 100, 107–110, 112, 115–116, 124
Cartesianism 40, 50, 92n2, 125
Cezanne, Paul 47–48
chronolytic *see* addictogenic
chronopathology *see* psychopathology
civilization 99–100, 102, 125

## 130  Index

cognition 6, 22, 66, 112; and recognition 17, 57, 101
cognitive science 5, 73–74, 76–77, 89
collective 27, 31, 60–61, 66, 78, 96–97, 99, 105–106, 110, 112–113
conscious 24, 27, 83; conscious awareness 91, 110, 123; conscious connection 87; conscious experience 23; conscious knowledge 83, 115, 118; consciousness 15, 23–28, 32, 37, 50, 75, 79, 81, 83, 110–112, 123; conscious reflection 35; conscious self-reflection 59; conscious subject 27, 83; conscious thought 126; conscious time 82–83; conscious understanding 111, 115; and self-consciousness 24, 27
conservatism 3, 5
consumer 10, 43, 86–87, 112–113; consumerism 10, 97, 12; and consumption 43–44, 97, 105, 107, 109, 112–113, 118
counter-transference *see* transference
critique 2, 15, 61, 106–107
Curtis, Adam 97; and *Century of the Self* 97
Cybernetics 73–74, 76–77

Da-sein 41–42, 60, 75, 78–80, 97, 107–110
de Man, Paul 2
deferral 22–24, 28; and différer 22, 28
Deleuze, Gilles 3
delusion 86, 100
Derrida, Jacques: *Dissemination* 3, 103; "Freud and the Scene of Writing" 4, 80; *Glas* 3, 87; *Of Grammatology* 21, 23, 53, 71, 75; *The Post Card* 3, 29; *Specters of Marx* 60; *Speech and Phenomena* 23, 25, 53; *The Truth in Painting* 7, 48; "Tympan" 87; and *Writing and Difference* 53
Descartes, René 74
desire 3, 28, 42–43, 47, 85, 87, 97–98, 100, 104, 110, 112–113, 115–118, 121
destruction 3, 112
Destruktion *see* destruction
desymbolization *see* symbolization
dialectic 6, 32, 40, 53–54, 56, 62, 71, 87
Dick, Kirby 1
différance 5–6, 13, 21–23, 28–30, 32, 35–36, 40, 46, 60, 63, 66, 116–117; and différer 22, 28–29
differentiation 20, 23–25, 28, 35, 37, 46, 62, 68n4, 85, 110, 115; and non-differentiation 19, 59
disclosure 40, 80, 107, 109–110
disruption 39, 58, 62–63, 66, 82, 127

dissemination 26, 28
dissociation 25
distortion 83–84, 86
dream 30–31, 57, 117, 121–123, 125
drive 5, 57, 105, 116, 125

echo 88–90
economic 5, 10, 42, 86, 97, 100–102, 105, 108
ecstatic 41–42, 49, 51, 78, 80, 82, 87, 89–91, 107, 112, 128
ego 11, 16–18, 25, 42, 59–60, 126
empathy 5, 57, 127
*en abyme* 4, 48, 52, 58; and *mise-en-ebyme* 53
energy 5, 30, 44, 64; and energy discharge 5
enunciation 22, 27
erasure 2, 23, 76, 112, 128
ergon *see* parergon
essence 40, 66, 73–76, 85, 89, 95–96, 100, 114, 117
ethics 105, 109–110, 113
exteriority 23–25
external 15, 17, 25–26, 28, 34, 49, 51, 61, 78, 96, 100–112, 115; and externalization 64, 66, 87

Fabozzi, Paolo 93n5
Faimberg, Haydée 53
fantasy 17, 30–32, 51, 56, 96, 98, 122, 125
Ferry, Luc 2
Ferro, Antonio 92n3
fetishism 117, 124, 127
Feurerbach, Ludwig 61
fixation 31, 90
force 5, 24, 28
Foucault, Michel 2–3
France 2, 53
free association 7, 51, 81, 84, 87, 90, 92n1, 118
Freedman, Norbert 86
French Philosophy of the Sixties (*La Penseé '68*) 2
Freud, Sigmund 2–5, 7–9, 16, 25, 27–29, 40–41, 47, 50–51, 57, 60, 63–65, 67n2, 68n6, 71, 78–81, 83–84, 89, 91, 92n2, 97, 99–100, 102–108, 116–117, 122–128; *Beyond the Pleasure Principle* 29; *Civilization and Its Discontents* 8, 97, 99, 105; The Freudian Pair 81; "Note on the Mystic Writing Pad" 4; *Project for a Scientific Psychology* 4; "Recommendations to physicians" 79, 81, 122; *Seeleapparat* 127; "Telepathy" 4, 7, 71, 79; techniques in the

Index **131**

art of living 8, 99–100, 102; and "The Uncanny" 4

Gasché, Rodolphe 127
Geisteskrankheit *see* spiritual sickness
Germanism 2
ghosts 7, 60–62; ghostly 56, 62–63, 88; and ghost world 52–53, 55–56, 59–63
Gill, Merton 5
grammē 76
Green, André 93n4

happiness 31, 100–102, 105
Harris, Adrienne 67n3
Hegel, Georg 9, 74, 92n2
Heidegger, Martin 2–3, 6–9, 22, 24, 35–36, 41–42, 48, 53, 58–60, 63–65, 71–80, 82, 87–90, 95–97, 103, 106–114, 116, 124; "The Anaximander Fragment" 77; *Being and Time* 41, 58, 65, 71, 78, 80, 87, 106–108; *Beïtrage zur Philosophie (Vom Ereignis)* 65; *Kant and the Problem of Metaphysics* 71, 79, 109; "The Origin of the Work of Art" 48; "The Question Concerning Technology" 95; "thinking" 7, 9, 13–14, 21, 35, 41–42, 50–51, 53, 65–66, 71–77, 79, 82, 84–87, 89–91, 95–97, 107–108, 110–111; and *What is Called Thinking?* 88
here-and-now 31, 42–43, 83, 86, 89–91
humanism 2, 5, 124–126
humanity 96–97, 100, 127
Husserl, Edmund 23, 74, 78, 107, 111
hypercathexis 65–66
hypnosis 57, 117

identity 13, 19, 23, 25, 27–28, 36, 44, 53, 76, 114; identity politics 3; self-identity 15, 24, 26; and subjective identity 42
illusion 29, 32–33, 45–46, 49, 52, 56, 73
imagination 1, 78–79
independence 100, 104–105
individuation 19, 33, 35–37, 42, 52, 66, 80, 85, 106, 128; and individuality 37, 99, 113
industrialization 10, 43, 99, 103
inheritance 60–61, 64, 92n1, 106
inner experience; 14–15, 28; inner space 15, 25–26, 33; and inner time 15
institution 7, 10, 52, 60–62, 64, 116
instruction 33, 84, 99
integration 14, 46, 53, 84, 86, 109, 112–114, 116
interiority 6, 15, 25, 27, 115

internal 15–16, 20–21, 23–25, 34, 49, 51, 61–62, 78–79; and internalization 29, 43, 64, 66, 87
International Psychoanalytic Association (IPA) 3–4
interpersonal 14, 27, 40, 42, 61, 86, 118
interpretation 14, 20, 29–32, 38, 40–41, 44–46, 52, 54–58, 61–62, 84–86, 90, 109–110, 113, 118, 127
intersubjective 28, 32–33, 40, 55, 62, 71, 81–83, 87, 90
interval 22, 24, 26, 36, 47, 49
intervention 8, 33–34, 83, 86, 118, 122
intoxication 52, 100, 104
introjection 16
irrational *see* rationality

Joyce, James 4

Kant, Immanuel 24, 74, 78–79; *Critique of Pure Reason* 79
Kierkegaard, Søren 95–96; and *The Sickness Unto Death* 95
Klein, Melanie 16, 45, 103, 114; and Kleinian 8, 20, 71, 89
knowledge 5, 37, 59, 61, 74, 82–84, 86, 101–102, 109, 114–115, 118; conscious knowledge *see* consciousness; maternal knowledge 114–115; objective knowledge 42; predetermined knowledge 43; self-knowledge 35, 51; and theoretical knowledge 59
Kohut, Heinz 127
Kraus, Karl 103

Lacan, Jacques 2–4, 10n1, 76, 93n4, 127
language 8, 17, 21, 26, 36, 75–76, 78, 84, 86, 88–89, 118, 121, 123; and linguistics 21, 23, 66, 77, 86
Laplanche, Jean 93n4
libido 100, 102, 105, 114; libidinal economies 99, 105–106; libidinal impulse 29; libidinal and investment 114, 117
literacy 37, 112, 123
Loewald, Hans 7–8, 15, 64–66, 87, 105; and *Sublimation* 64
love 100, 113, 115, 121

machine 5, 43, 76–78, 121, 124–127; and writing machine 5, 80
Mahler, Margaret; Pine, Fred; & Bergman, Anni 67n4
Mallarmé, Stephane 4

## 132 Index

Marcuse, Herbert 106, 125
Marx, Karl 9, 61; and Marxism 61
material inscription 60, 75–76, 104, 107, 111, 115
materiality 61, 65, 77, 89
maternalism 5
memory 7, 16, 44, 47, 60, 63, 76, 78, 82, 85, 87, 104, 106, 110–113, 115, 117, 122–123; and memorization 51, 104, 111, 119n2
mental health 35, 51, 83, 103, 106, 117–118, 128
mental illness 103
metaphysics 3, 15, 25–26, 59, 64, 72–73, 75–78, 81–82, 89, 91, 105, 109, 124, 127; metaphysical opposition 27–28, 55, 66, 77, 117; metaphysics of presence 15, 23, 40, 90–9; non-metaphysical 6–7, 40, 67, 78, 110; and Western metaphysics 31
metapsychology 33
Milner, Marion 7, 44–48, 52–58, 62–63; and framed gap 44–45, 47, 52, 55, 57
mirror 43, 58, 88–89, 127; and mirroring 89
Mitchell, Stephen A. 30
mother-infant matrix 6, 18–20, 30, 83; and mother-and-infant dyad 18; and mother-infant relationship 9, 19, 29, 33; mother-infant unity 18–19; and maternal 5, 20, 89, 113–115, 118

narcissism 18, 43, 49, 64, 88–90, 105, 109, 119n1, 123, 127
narrative 14, 28, 31
Nazism 2
neutrality 38, 40–41, 60, 81–82, 87, 96, 118; neutral analyst 46; and neutral frame 40, 44, 61
*The New York Times* 1
neutral reverie 83–84
Nietzsche, Friedrick 2–3, 9, 41, 53, 60, 74, 108, 124
nihilism 104, 109
non-interpersonal *see* interpersonal
non-process 54–58
nostalgia 99

objective presence 41–42, 58–59, 63, 78, 107–108
objectivity 41, 56, 61, 89
Ogden, Thomas 6, 13, 18–20, 26, 29, 56, 92n2; and *The Matrix of the Mind* 13
ontology 32, 34–36, 40, 48, 56, 60, 106–110, 114
origin 23, 25, 72, 74–76, 117

other 5, 13–14, 17–19, 21, 23, 32–33, 36, 38, 46, 51, 55–56, 61–62, 75, 77, 79, 82–83, 87–90, 118, 126–127

parergon 48–49, 51
passivity 7, 14, 20, 22, 24, 26, 41, 48, 49, 51–52, 60, 65, 74–75, 78, 81–82, 127
pathology 35, 42; and psychopathology 16, 90–91, 112
pessimism 99–102, 105–106
Peterson, Jordan 2
Pharmacology 95, 103, 105–106, 116, 118; pharmaceutical 57, 104, 107, 117; pharmaka 8, 104, 107; and pharmakon 104–105, 117
phenomenology 23, 25, 107
phonē 23, 76
Plato 74, 103–104; Platonic 3, 73, 105; and *Phaedrus* 103–104
pleasure 43, 64–65, 100–102; and pleasure principle 29, 105, 116
Plotnitsky, Arkady 27–28
politics 3, 9–10, 42, 61, 77, 97, 106–107, 109–110, 112–113
possession 23, 35–37, 41–42, 56, 60, 65, 72, 81, 89, 92, 110, 112, 128
postmodernism 2
presence 18, 22, 24, 26–27, 29, 31, 45, 47, 49, 55, 60–61, 63, 65, 73–75, 77–78, 89, 91, 106, 110–111, 122, 128
projection *see* introjection
psyche 16, 18, 25, 28, 30, 66, 77, 90–91, 125–126
psychic interiority 6, 27
psychic space 5, 13, 16, 21, 23, 25, 27–28, 30, 34, 115

rationality 5, 50, 74, 96, 124; and rationalization 76
reality principle *see* pleasure; and pleasure principle
Reason 74, 76
receptivity 82
reduction 21, 23–25, 40, 75, 86–87, 101, 108
reflection 7, 14–16, 18, 20–21, 24, 26, 35, 50, 53, 59, 71–72, 76, 89, 91, 95, 104, 109–110, 117, 124, 127, 128; and self-reflection 15, 24, 26, 59, 68n4, 127
relationality 35, 37, 42, 78, 118; relational 40, 42, 46, 62, 81–82, 86, 89, 91, 116, 118; and self-relation 23–24, 26, 78
reminiscence 99
Renaut, Alain 2
renunciation 100, 116

Index **133**

repetition 15, 37–40, 43, 46, 55–56, 60–61, 66, 74, 81–82, 85, 89–91, 113
representation 5, 15, 27, 32–33, 52, 56, 59, 61, 63, 66, 72, 75, 77, 96, 110, 123; and representation-calculation 73–74, 76, 79, 87, 89, 96
repression 23, 25, 27
resonance 63–66, 87–88, 90–91, 92n2, 127
retention 82, 111; primary retention 111; secondary retention 111; and tertiary retention 111–112, 115
retreat 20, 49, 52, 58, 79, 83, 90, 125
retrospective 82, 91, 99
reverberation 83–84, 87–89, 91
reverie 83–84, 87, 90, 92
Roudinesco, Elisabeth 2–3, 117–118, 124; and *Why Psychoanalysis?* 117

Saussure, Ferdinand 21, 23, 68n5
*Seinfeld* 1
self-expression 97
self-presence 15, 23–27, 51, 75, 83, 112
self-reference 23–24
separation 18, 111
session 38, 44–46, 55, 81, 84, 118, 122
signified *see* signifier
signifier 21–25, 49, 51, 76, 104; and signify 23, 61, 66
sorge *see* care
space-time 41, 60, 89, 91
spacing 21–22, 26–27, 32, 36, 47, 86
spectrality 6–7, 53, 60, 77; spectral 53, 62–67, 91, 113; spectral ghost 60; spectral materiality 61, 63; spectral technology 7; and spectral vocabulary 64, 117
speech 24, 77, 88–89, 123, 125
spiritual sickness 103
splitting 20, 25, 99, 108, 116
Stiegler, Bernard 8–9, 103, 105–107, 110–116, 118, 119n1–n2; *Taking Care of Youth and the Generations* 112; *Technics and Time* 106, 110, 113; and *What Makes Life Worth Living: On Pharmacology* 113
stimulation 29, 64–65
strategy 4, 6, 35, 57, 125
subjectivity 20, 41, 61, 79, 86, 89, 91, 96, 109, 125
subjugation 96, 101–102
sublimation 65, 105–106
suffering 98–99, 103, 105, 118
suggestion 84, 117
surrealism 4
symbolization 6, 14, 18, 20, 31–33, 36, 40, 46, 63–66, 82, 85–87, 91, 110, 127; symbol 17–18, 20–21, 85, 14, 40; symbolic activity 29; symbolic equation 20, 85; symbolic misery 116–116; symbolic order 116; symbolic thinking 84, 86; symbolizing 5, 9, 14, 32–33, 36, 40, 86; desymbolizing 88; and unsymbolized experience

talking cure 47, 84–85
technology 7–8, 39, 60, 65, 67, 73–75, 89, 95–97, 102, 104, 107, 127; technics 9, 75, 79, 96–97, 100, 106–107, 110, 119n1; technique 4, 8–9, 32, 37–39, 52, 54, 57, 60, 71, 82–84, 86, 97, 99–100, 102–103, 105–107, 113–118; and techno-science 73, 76, 102
telepathy 7, 89, 91, 122, 124; and telepathic 79–80, 82, 89, 91, 121, 123
temporality 28, 42–43, 54, 78, 81–87, 90–91; temporal collage 81–82; temporalization 14, 29; and temporization 26, 36
therapeutic 10, 14, 29, 37–40, 45, 84, 86–87, 107, 113; therapeutic action 34–35, 40, 85; therapeutic intervention 33, 118; therapeutic practice 9, 54; therapeutic procedure 54, 57; therapeutic process 14, 30–31; therapeutic relationship 30, 33; therapeutic technique 9, 32, 38, 52, 86, 106–107, 118; and therapeutic transformation 40, 52, 66
Theuth 104
time-space 40, 45–46
trace 1, 5, 7, 19, 22, 24, 26, 28, 36, 51, 65, 72, 76, 87–88, 91, 98, 107, 111–112, 126–128
transference 8, 14, 21, 33, 38, 40, 45–46, 52, 62, 84–86, 90, 118, 122–123, 125
transference interpretation *see* transference
transformation 8, 15, 35, 40, 52, 66, 72, 74–75, 84–86, 88–90, 99, 109, 118
transitional: transitional area 33; transitional character 114; transitionality 6, 89; transitional object 19, 45, 113–117, 119n1–n2; transitional phenomena 16, 45, 89, 113–117, 119n1–n2; transitional region 18; transitional space 16, 18, 60, 88–89, 91, 116; transitional space-time *see* transitional space; and transitional time-space 40
translation 2, 35, 37, 80–81
transmission 79–80, 82, 91, 97, 105
trauma 17–18, 98, 113, 121, 127–128
Tylim, Isaac 67n3

**134** Index

uncanniness 42, 63, 79–80; and uncanny 82, 115, 123

unconscious 7, 16, 25, 27–28, 32–33, 43, 54, 60, 79–83, 88–89, 91, 106, 108, 122–123, 125–126; becoming-unconscious 27; Freudian unconscious 5, 107, 126; unconscious communication 71, 80–81, 83, 89; unconscious fantasy 56; unconscious memory 16; unconsciousness 28, 32; unconscious order 82; and unconscious processes 79, 110

unpleasure *see* pleasure

urge 107–109

valorization 15, 49, 74–75, 77, 87, 117, 125

Winnicott, Donald 6, 9, 15–20, 26, 29–33, 45, 49, 54, 56, 58, 64, 88–89, 92n2, 93n4,
113–117, 119n1–n2, 127; "Hate in the Countertransference" 93n5; play 17, 28–33, 47, 76, 89, 115–118, 126; playing 6, 17, 29–32, 45, 115–117; and *Playing and Reality* 16; and "Transitional Objects and Transitional Phenomena" 16

wish 17, 29, 107, 123; and wish-world 106–110, 112, 116, 118

withdrawal 22, 47, 56, 100

work of art 7, 48–50, 52; and "The Origin of the Work of Art" 48

writing 4–7, 28, 29, 36–37, 46–47, 51, 53, 60, 65–66, 71–72, 75–77, 80–81, 85, 87–89, 104–105, 110, 112, 123, 125–128; and arche-writing 76, 91, 111

Ziering, Amy 1

Žižek, Slavoj 2